THE GREATNESS
OF
THE DAY OF THE LORD
AND
CHRIST'S KINGDOM

BY
DAVID OLANDER

The Greatness of the Day of the Lord and Christ's Kingdom

©2017 Tyndale Seminary Press

by David Olander, Ph.D, Th.D

Published by Tyndale Seminary Press
Hurst, TX

ISBN10 – 1542751748

ISBN13 – 978-1542751742

The day of the Lord beginning with His wrath is coming upon a God rejecting world!

"Alas for the day! For the day of the LORD is near, and it will come as destruction from the Almighty" (Joel 1:15)

"For the day of the LORD draws near on all the nations. As you have done, it will be done to you. Your dealings will return on your own head" (Obadiah 1:15)

"Near is the great day of the LORD, near and coming very quickly; listen, the day of the LORD! In it the warrior cries out bitterly. A day of wrath is that day, A day of trouble and distress, A day of destruction and desolation, A day of darkness and gloom, A day of clouds and thick darkness" (Zeph. 1:14)

"Wail, for the day of the LORD is near! It will come as destruction from the Almighty" (Isaiah 13:6)

The church will be raptured prior to the day of the Lord!

"For you yourselves know full well that the day of the Lord will come just like a thief in the night" (1Thess. 5:2)

"Now we request you, brethren, with regard to the coming of our Lord Jesus Christ, and our gathering together to Him, that you may not be quickly shaken from your composure or be disturbed either by a spirit or a message or a letter as if from us, to the effect that the day of the Lord has come" (2 Thes. 2:1-2)

The Lord will return and bring in His covenanted kingdom after His wrath in the day of the Lord!

"And it will come about in that day That the mountains will drip with sweet wine, And the hills will flow with milk, And all the brooks of Judah will flow with water; And a spring will go out from the house of the LORD, To water the valley of Shittim" (Joel 3:18)

"The LORD has taken away His judgments against you; He has cleared away your enemies. The King of Israel, the LORD, is in your midst; you will fear disaster no more. In that day it will be said to Jerusalem: "Do not be afraid, O Zion; do not let your hands fall limp. The LORD your God is in your midst, a victorious warrior. He will exult over you with joy, He will be quiet in His love, He will rejoice over you with shouts of joy" (Zeph. 3:15-17)

Table of Contents

The day of the Lord
An Introduction to the day of the Lord

"Alas for the day! For the day of the LORD is near,
and it will come as destruction from the Almighty"
(Joel 1:15).

The day of the Lord is biblical doctrine

The day of the Lord is major biblical doctrine in both the Old and New Testaments. The day of the Lord is such an extremely crucial doctrine that it is referenced well over one hundred times in all the Text. There are so many references to the day of Lord in all Scripture it was known as that day, the day, the days, a day, the great day, a unique day, and several other similar designations.[1] It is such an important doctrine that without a proper understanding of the day of the Lord, the prophetic word especially biblical eschatology cannot and will not be properly understood.

The following is a sampling of the various designations referred to as the day of the Lord. For a more comprehensive list see the appendices at the end of the book.

1) Joel 1:15 "Alas for the day! For the day of the LORD is near, and it will come as destruction from the Almighty."

2) Joel 2:31 "The sun will be turned into darkness, and the moon into blood, before the great and awesome day of the LORD comes."

3) Zephaniah 1:14 "Near is the great day of the LORD, near and coming very quickly; Listen, the day of the LORD! In it the warrior cries out bitterly."

4) Zephaniah 1:15 "A day of wrath is that day, A day of trouble and distress, A day of destruction and desolation,

---

[1] See appendices A, B, and C on the various uses of the term 'the day of the Lord.' These appendices include various associated phrases concerning 'the day of the Lord.' Actually there are more but it is difficult to include all of them.

<u>A day</u> of darkness and gloom, <u>A day</u> of clouds and thick darkness."

5) Isaiah 61:2 "To proclaim the favorable year of the LORD, and <u>the day of vengeance</u> of our God; to comfort all who mourn."

6) Isaiah 24:21 "So it will happen in <u>that day</u>, That the LORD will punish the host of heaven, on high, And the kings of the earth, on earth."

7) Isaiah 27:6 "In <u>the days</u> to come Jacob will take root, Israel will blossom and sprout; and they will fill the whole world with fruit."

8) Isaiah 27:13 "It will come about also in <u>that day</u> that a great trumpet will be blown; and those who were perishing in the land of Assyria and who were scattered in the land of Egypt will come and worship the LORD in the holy mountain at Jerusalem."

9) Ezekiel 38:14 "Therefore, prophesy, son of man, and say to Gog, 'Thus says the Lord God, "On <u>that day</u> when My people Israel are living securely, will you not know it?"

10) Ezekiel 39:11 "And it will come about on <u>that day</u> that I shall give Gog a burial ground there in Israel, the valley of those who pass by east of the sea, and it will block off the passers-by. So they will bury Gog there with all his multitude, and they will call it the valley of Hamon-gog."

11) Hosea 2:18 "In <u>that day</u> I will also make a covenant for them with the beasts of the field, the birds of the sky, and the creeping things of the ground. And I will abolish the bow, the sword, and war from the land, and will make them lie down in safety."

12) Obadiah 1:15 "For <u>the day of the LORD</u> draws near on all the nations. As you have done, it will be done to you. Your dealings will return on your own head."

13) Zechariah 12:3 "And it will come about in <u>that day</u> that I will make Jerusalem a heavy stone for all the peoples; all who lift it will be severely injured. And all the nations of the earth will be gathered against it."

14) Malachi 4:5 "Behold, I am going to send you Elijah the prophet before <u>the coming of the great and terrible day of the LORD</u>."
15) Zechariah 14:7 "For it will be <u>a unique day</u> which is known to the LORD, neither day nor night, but it will come about that at evening time there will be light."

A study of the day of the Lord

This was simply an introduction to the biblical doctrine of the day of the Lord. An in-depth study of the day of the Lord is vital for understanding biblical truth especially concerning biblical prophecy. It is therefore necessary to study the most important prophets and their teachings presenting the doctrine of the day of the Lord. Chapter 1 will present absolute essentials for an understanding of this doctrine. Chapter 2 will begin a sequential study of the individual prophets beginning with Joel. Joel's prophecy is fundamental for this study as this prophet accurately defines the day of the Lord. The following chapters will include Obadiah, Zephaniah, Zechariah, and various other prophets dealing with this doctrine.

In the New Testament Paul taught the day of the Lord as an essential feature of his eschatology. There will be other New Testament references especially those in Revelation. All this is prayerfully presented so the reader will gain a true understanding of the biblical truth concerning the day of the Lord.

10　　Day of the Lord

Chapter 1
The day of the Lord

The day of the Lord includes many issues

The day of the Lord is a very inclusive doctrine and precisely developed throughout the entire Old Testament. The day of the Lord is so comprehensive with so many components that there are entire Texts dedicated to this doctrine i.e. Joel, Obadiah, and Zephaniah. Joel the first of the writing prophets especially to the southern kingdom defines the day of the Lord. Obadiah who singles out Edom and its hatred of Jacob and Jerusalem deals directly with the day of the Lord.[1] Most all the prophets warn of the coming day of the Lord and some more extensively such as Zechariah.[2]

Paul, in the New Testament, clearly explains that the church cannot possibly go into the day of the Lord in both 1st and 2nd Thessalonians.[3] The latter was written solely to give

---

[1] See the dating of Obadiah in the section titled Obadiah. Some date Obadiah very early and others quite late. In either case this really does not make much difference as Obadiah deals directly with the day of the Lord and the warnings of the coming devastation on the nations.

[2] In Zechariah alone 'that day' is used over 20 times and appears that each use is much referenced to the day of the Lord.

[3] Note that both 1st and 2nd Thessalonians deal with the day of the Lord. And both prove a pre-day of the Lord rapture. So very important for the church to understand this. "For they themselves report about us what kind of a reception we had with you, and how you turned to God from idols to serve a living and true God, and to wait for His Son from heaven, whom He raised from the dead, *that is* Jesus, **who delivers us from the wrath to come**" (1Thes. 1:9-10); "For who is our hope or joy or crown of exultation? Is it not even you, in **the presence of our Lord Jesus at His coming?**" (1Thes. 2:19)**; "**So that He may establish your hearts unblamable in holiness before our God and Father **at the coming of our Lord Jesus with all His saints**" (1Thes. 3:13); "For the Lord Himself will descend from heaven with a shout, with the voice of *the* archangel, and with the trumpet of God; and the dead in Christ shall rise first. **Then we who are alive and remain shall be caught up together with them in the clouds to meet the Lord in the air**, and thus we shall always be with the Lord" (1Thess. 4:16-17); *(**The preceding is the rapture of the church i.e. the meeting with the Lord Jesus in the air then**

specific details that the church cannot possibly go into the day of the Lord.

The day of the Lord begins with His future divine wrath.

> "Alas for the day! For the day of the LORD is near, and it will come as destruction[4] from the Almighty" (Joel 1:15); "For the day of the LORD draws near on all the nations. As you have done, it will be done to you. Your dealings will return on your own head. "Because just as you drank on My holy mountain, All the nations will drink continually. They will drink and swallow, and become as if they had never existed" (Obadiah 1:15-16); 'Near is the great day of the LORD, Near and coming very quickly; Listen, the day of the LORD! In it the warrior cries out bitterly. A day of wrath is that day, A day of trouble and distress, A day of destruction and desolation, A day of darkness and gloom, A day of clouds and thick darkness" (Zeph. 1:14-15).

**the day of the Lord which begins with His coming wrath 1 Thes. 1:10))**
"Now as to the times and the epochs, brethren, you have no need of anything to be written to you. **For you yourselves know full well that <u>the day of the Lord will come just like a thief in the night</u>**. While they are saying, "Peace and safety!" then destruction will come upon them suddenly like birth pangs upon a woman with child; and they shall not escape. But you, brethren, are not in darkness, that the day should overtake you like a thief; for you are all sons of light and sons of day. We are not of night nor of darkness" (1Thes. 5:1-5). "Now we request you, brethren, with regard to the coming of our Lord Jesus Christ, and our gathering together to Him, **that you may not be quickly shaken from your composure or be disturbed either by a spirit or a message or a letter as if from us, to the effect that <u>the day of the Lord has come</u>**. Let no one in any way deceive you, for _it will not come_ unless the apostasy comes first, and the man of lawlessness is revealed, the son of destruction" (2 Thes. 2:1-3).

[4] שֹׁד **n.m.** violence, havoc, devastation, ruin; BDB p. 494.

All the above refers to a future day of His coming wrath. This specifically defined wrath is only in the day of the Lord. Paul made it very clear to the Thessalonians that they (the church) could and would not possibly go into this time of wrath.[5] "For they themselves report about us what kind of a reception we had with you, and how you turned to God from idols to serve a living and true God, and to wait for His Son from heaven, whom He raised from the dead, *that is* Jesus, who delivers us from the wrath to come" (1Thess. 1:9-10). This wrath is exclusively in the day of the Lord. But this is only one aspect concerning the day of the Lord.

The day of the Lord includes the seventieth week of Daniel, a great tribulation, the pouring out of the Holy Spirit, the regeneration of Israel, the second coming of Christ, Jesus' assumption of the covenanted Davidic throne in Jerusalem, His covenanted kingdom for 1,000 years, final judgments, and much more.

The day of the Lord includes

I.   The 70th week of Daniel (Dan. 9:24-27)
II.   A great tribulation (defined by Christ at approximately half way through the 70th week of Daniel (Mat. 24:15-21)[6]

---

[5] For more information on the rapture see this author's book 'The Greatness of the Rapture.' The subtitle is 'The Pre-day of the Lord Rapture'
[6] These are Christ's very own words: "for then there will be a great tribulation, such as has not occurred since the beginning of the world until now, nor ever shall" (Mat. 24:21); This parallels or fits in with the day of Lord as described by Joel. "Blow a trumpet in Zion, and sound an alarm on My holy mountain! Let all the inhabitants of the land tremble, For the day of the LORD is coming; Surely it is near, A day of darkness and gloom, A day of clouds and thick darkness. As the dawn is spread over the mountains, *So* there is a great and mighty people; There has never been *anything* like it, Nor will there be again after it To the years of many generations" (Joel 2:1-2). Yet this period is limited in time and occurs in the last half of the 70th week of Daniel.

III.   The pouring out of the Holy Spirit before the climatic and final phase of the day of the Lord (Joel 2:28-32)

IV.   The second coming of Christ (Mat. 24:29-30; Rev. 19:11-16)[7]

V.   The binding of Satan (Rev. 20:1-3)

VI.   Jesus takes the covenanted Davidic throne (Mat. 19:28; 25:31-33)

VII.   His kingdom begins with the sheep and goats judgments (Mat. 25:31-46)

VIII.   The Messianic kingdom and reign for 1,000 years (Rev. 20:1-4)

IX.   The final revolt of Satan and man (Rev. 20:7-9)

X.   The final judgments prior to the eternal state (Rev. 20:10-15)

XI.   The transfer of the kingdom to the eternal state (1 Cor. 15:24-25)

XII.   The eternal state (Rev. 21-22)

All the preceding components need to be understood in biblical context and accurately noting all the associated details.[8] In context there is much more information being presented with each issue as all of these are very unique and biblically defined. There is much to be discerned as there are so many details. As the 70th week of Daniel, the great tribulation, the second coming of Christ, the coming kingdom, and much more are in the day of the Lord, each one has very defined beginnings and time periods.

---

[7] Technically, Christ returns towards the end of a great tribulation which is in the day of the Lord (Mat. 24:15-30).

[8] What many studies do not get into are the many details in context. As this effects many areas of biblical truth, this seems more so with biblical prophecy.

The day of the Lord begins with His coming wrath

The day of the Lord which includes His future eschatological wrath[9] should not be confused with particular divine wrath which has come in different ways even today (Rom. 1:18-19).[10] What is of major concern is the day of the Lord, specifically His future wrath defined biblically.

The day of the Lord begins primarily with His eschatological wrath coming as a thief in the night on an unsuspecting and unbelieving world. Paul warned of this coming wrath to the church at Thessalonica. But His wrath cannot possibly come upon the Thessalonians for the church has to be raptured before the day of the Lord even begins. "Now as to the times and the epochs, brethren, you have no need of anything to be written to you. For you yourselves know full well that the day of the Lord will come just like a thief in the night. While they are saying, 'Peace and safety!' then destruction will come upon them suddenly like birth pangs upon a woman with child; and they shall not escape" (1 Thess. 5:1-3). Note while they (not the Thessalonians) are saying peace and safety then destruction will come upon them. The Thessalonians (or the church) is not and cannot be included with this coming wrath and destruction.

It must be noted that the church cannot go into the day of the Lord in any sense, and this is made perfectly clear in the Scriptures. The day of the Lord is biblically defined wrath

---

[9]This is His future eschatological wrath which is biblical defined and very precise in its nature and extent. "For the wrath of God is <u>revealed</u> from heaven against all ungodliness and unrighteousness of men, who suppress the truth in unrighteousness, because that which is known about God is evident within them; for God made it evident to them" (Rom. 1:18-19). There is a certain divine wrath that is revealed but this is not His eschatological wrath in the day of the Lord. Ἀποκαλύπτεται (present passive indicative.. and this is very significant as this divine wrath is being continuously revealed) γὰρ ὀργὴ θεοῦ ἀπ' οὐρανοῦ ἐπὶ πᾶσαν ἀσέβειαν καὶ ἀδικίαν ἀνθρώπων τῶν τὴν ἀλήθειαν ἐν ἀδικίᾳ κατεχόντων' (Rom 1:18).

[10] Divine wrath can be of a local judgment or even worldwide but this is not to be confused with a specific time coming on the whole of creation defined as 'the day of the Lord.' (see above footnote)

which will be poured out on a God rejecting world and Satan's eschatological kingdom. There is coming upon an unbelieving world the Lord's complete and total destruction. This has never happened to the extent which is prophesied in these verses or any verses referring to the day of the Lord. The day of the Lord includes His divine eschatological wrath and is major bible doctrine.

There are many references to the day of the Lord and His coming wrath

There are many other references in Scripture to the day of the Lord, and each follows much defined parameters referring to that day as an extended period of time when His wrath will be released on an unbelieving world. The day of the Lord will come upon the world unexpectedly and as a thief in the night (1 Thess. 5:2). This very specific time of divine wrath has various designations.   These include 'in that day, the day of the Lord's anger, the time of Jacob's trouble or distress'[11] and many more. "Peter describes the suddenness of the coming of the day of the Lord (2 Pet. 3:10). The day of the Lord is used in several ways in Scripture, but as a general term it views the entire period beginning with the rapture and terminating at the end of the millennium; thus, the day of the Lord involves judgment upon unbelievers but blessing for believers. From 2 Peter 3:10b–12 Peter describes the eternal state. At the end of the millennium the heavens will pass away with a great noise and the earth will be burned up. This is the sphere where sin took place; it is renovated in anticipation of eternity. Peter concludes his study on last things with a practical exhortation (2 Pet. 3:11)."[12]

---

[11]Jeremiah 30:7 'Alas! For that day is great, there is none like it; And it is the time of Jacob's distress, But he will be saved from it.'

[12] Paul Enns, *The Moody Handbook of Theology* (Chicago, IL.: Moody Press, 1989), 129.

Major biblical references
concerning the day of the Lord
and His coming wrath

1) Isa. 13:6 Wail, for the _day of the Lord_ is near! It will come as destruction from the Almighty.

2) Isa. 13:9 Behold, the _day of the Lord_ is coming, Cruel, with fury and burning anger, To make the land a desolation; And He will exterminate its sinners from it.

3) Ezek. 13:5 "You have not gone up into the breaches, nor did you build the wall around the house of Israel to stand in the battle on the _day of the Lord_.

4) Ezek. 30:3 "For the day is near, Even the _day of the Lord_ is near; It will be a day of clouds, A time of doom for the nations.

5) Joel 1:15 Alas for the day! For the _day of the Lord_ is near, And it will come as destruction from the Almighty.

6) Joel 2:1 Blow a trumpet in Zion, And sound an alarm on My holy mountain! Let all the inhabitants of the land tremble, For the _day of the Lord_ is coming; Surely it is near,

7) Joel 2:11 And the Lord utters His voice before His army; Surely His camp is very great, For strong is he who carries out His word. The _day of the Lord_ is indeed great and very awesome, And who can endure it?

8) Joel 2:31 "The sun will be turned into darkness, And the moon into blood, Before the great and awesome _day of the Lord_ comes.

9) Joel 3:14 Multitudes, multitudes in the valley of decision! For the _day of the Lord_ is near in the valley of decision.

10) Amos 5:18 Alas, you who are longing for the *day of the Lord*, For what purpose will the *day of the Lord* be to you? It will be darkness and not light;

11) Amos 5:20 Will not the *day of the Lord* be darkness instead of light, Even gloom with no brightness in it?

12) Obadiah 15 "For the *day of the Lord* draws near on all the nations. As you have done, it will be done to you. Your dealings will return on your own head.

13) Zeph. 1:7 Be silent before the Lord God! For the *day of the Lord* is near, For the Lord has prepared a sacrifice, He has consecrated His guests.

14) Zeph. 1:14-16 Near is the great *day of the Lord*, Near and coming very quickly; Listen, the *day of the Lord*! In it the warrior cries out bitterly. A day of wrath is that day, A day of trouble and distress, A day of destruction and desolation, A day of darkness and gloom, A day of clouds and thick darkness, A day of trumpet and battle cry, Against the fortified cities And the high corner towers.

15) Zeph. 1:18 Neither their silver nor their gold Will be able to deliver them On the *day of the Lord*'s wrath; And all the earth will be devoured In the fire of His jealousy, For He will make a complete end, Indeed a terrifying one, Of all the inhabitants of the earth.

16) Mal. 4:5 Behold, I am going to send you Elijah the prophet before the coming of the great and terrible *day of the Lord*.

17) Acts 2:20 The sun shall be turned into darkness, And the moon into blood, Before the great and glorious *day of the Lord* shall come.

18) 1 Cor. 5:5 I have decided to deliver such a one to Satan for the destruction of his flesh, that his spirit may be saved in the *day of the Lord* Jesus.

19) 1 Thess. 5:2 For you yourselves know full well that the *day of the Lord* will come just like a thief in the night.

20) 2 Thess. 2:2 That you may not be quickly shaken from your composure or be disturbed either by a spirit or a message or a letter as if from us, to the effect that the *day of the Lord* has come.

21) 2 Pet. 3:10 But the *day of the Lord* will come like a thief, in which the heavens will pass away with a roar and the elements will be destroyed with intense heat, and the earth and its works will be burned up.

Note the various terms used concerning the day of the Lord: destruction from the Almighty (several times), cruel, fury and burning anger, desolation, exterminate, doom for the nations, tremble, very great and awesome, who can endure, moon into blood, valley of decision, darkness instead of light, darkness and not light, prepared a sacrifice, trouble and distress, darkness and gloom, clouds and thick darkness, trumpet and battle cry, devoured in the fire of His jealousy, complete end, terrifying, destruction, roar and intense heat, etc. There are many other references in Scripture referring to this time of destruction and complete devastation from the Lord.

There is absolutely no doubt that the day of the Lord is a major doctrine of the Text. There should be no question that the biblical judgments in the day of the Lord have not happened especially to the degree as described in God's Word. To say these divine judgments have occurred in the past and are already fulfilled or perhaps are being fulfilled is a rather naïve and shallow view of the Text.[13] It also must be noted that the kingdom will come in the day of the Lord but not until all the judgments of that day are completed. Note well the judgments of the day of the Lord, only after that will be blessings for

---

[13] Any biblical position denying this coming time of complete divine wrath upon the world is truly a denial of the literal Text.

Israel, especially His kingdom. There is no kingdom until the day of the Lord. The church is in no sense a kingdom or is it helping Him to build His kingdom.

> "Put in the sickle, for the harvest is ripe. Come, tread, for the wine press is full; the vats overflow, for their wickedness is great. Multitudes, multitudes in the valley of decision! For the day of the LORD is near in the valley of decision. The sun and moon grow dark, and the stars lose their brightness. And the LORD roars from Zion and utters His voice from Jerusalem, and the heavens and the earth tremble. But the LORD is a refuge for His people and a stronghold to the sons of Israel. Then you will know that I am the LORD your God, Dwelling in Zion My holy mountain. So Jerusalem will be holy, and strangers will pass through it no more. And it will come about in that day that the mountains will drip with sweet wine, And the hills will flow with milk, And all the brooks of Judah will flow with water; And a spring will go out from the house of the LORD, To water the valley of Shittim. Egypt will become a waste, And Edom will become a desolate wilderness, Because of the violence done to the sons of Judah, In whose land they have shed innocent blood. But Judah will be inhabited forever, And Jerusalem for all generations. And I will avenge their blood which I have not avenged, For the LORD dwells in Zion" (Joel 3:13-21).

There are so many associated facets concerning all the above and the eternal state,[14] it is almost impossible to include all the details. The day of the Lord is a major bible doctrine

---

[14] All this will be developed in more detail.

which should be understood by every student of the Word of God. The day of the Lord might be classified as one of the least understood biblical teachings in the entire Text.

A study of the day of the Lord

The following chapters begin with the prophets especially Joel. Joel is the first of the writing prophets and he alone introduces the truth concerning the many features of the day of the Lord.

Chapter 2
The day of the Lord in Joel

"Alas for the day! For the day of the LORD is
near, and it will come as destruction from the
Almighty" (1:15).

The prophet Joel introduces the day of the Lord

The Old Testament prophets warned of the future day of
the Lord. Joel appears to be the first of the writing prophets.
He was also the first of the writing prophets to the southern
kingdom. "Joel means 'the Lord (*Yahweh*) is God.' The name
of his father is given, but merely to distinguish him from others
of the same name. He leaves even the time he prophesied to be
guessed at. Although modern critics date him late (post-Exilic)
conservative scholars place him as perhaps the earliest of the
minor prophets, during the reign of Joash (*c.* 800 B.C.)."[1]

It has already been established that the day of the Lord is
a major biblical and eschatological doctrine. The prophet Joel
is the key prophet who not only introduced the day of the Lord
but also defined the day of the Lord. He is the one who
introduced the term or this time period so any definition of the
day of the Lord must not only include Joel but *must* begin with
Joel.[2] All the other prophets will take this biblically defined
period and refer to it as that day, a day, the day, etc. especially
when referring to future judgments of His divine wrath and His
future kingdom blessings.

---

[1]Merrill Frederick Unger, *The New Unger's Bible Handbook*, Rev. and
updated ed. (Chicago: Moody Publishers, 2005), 324.

[2]The dating of Joel is important but not as important as realizing the true
Author of all Scripture is God the Holy Spirit. This author considers Joel as
perhaps the first of the writing prophets who truly defined the day of the
Lord. Most of the other prophets did use the term and interweave the term in
their writings, but this does not mean Joel did not give a technical definition
to the day of the Lord. The primary reason Joel was written was to define
the coming day of the Lord and its great and vast importance to the prophetic
Text especially concerning the coming judgments preceding the millennial
reign of the Lord Jesus Christ, the true King of Israel.

His future promised blessings include the pouring out of His Spirit on Israel, His second coming, His ascending to the Davidic throne, the restoration of the covenanted nation Israel for His kingdom, His kingdom reign for 1,000 years from Jerusalem, and so much more. All this can and will happen only in the day of the Lord. This is easily discerned from the context of almost all the Hebrews prophets in the Old Testament.   The day of the Lord is a time which begins with His unprecedented future divine wrath and culminates with His unprecedented future kingdom blessings which transfer into the eternal state. All this is not only included in the day of the Lord but defines the day of the Lord.

A local plague and the coming day of the Lord

Joel 1:1-12 begins with a locust plague which was a local plague occurring at that time. Whether this plague was of divine judgment or a natural disaster was not fully specified. It is not that significant for the prophet leaps from this local plague into a future time known or defined as the day of the Lord. "Natural disasters—from rising floodwaters to violent earthquakes—provoke fear and dread. With all their ingenuity, people still cannot control these powerful and destructive forces. They can only watch in awe. Joel begins his book with a description of such a natural disaster—a plague of ravenous locusts. In the prophet's hands, the destructiveness of this plague becomes a vivid warning of the power of God's coming judgment and a clear appeal to run to the Lord for mercy."[3] This can be summed up by the petition 'whoever calls on the name of the Lord will be delivered or saved (Joel 2:32).'[4]

---

[3] *The Nelson Ministry Services Bible.* (Nashville: Thomas Nelson Publishers, 1997), 1,464.

[4] "And it will come about that whoever calls on the name of the LORD Will be delivered; For on Mount Zion and in Jerusalem There will be those who escape, As the LORD has said, Even among the survivors whom the LORD calls" (Joel 2:32). This cry for deliverance will occur during the day of the Lord. It must be noted that 'whoever calls on Him for deliverance will be delivered. מָלַט niphal. ...2. *escape*, Francis Brown, Samuel Rolles Driver

Joel used this local disaster as a warning or harbinger of future judgments that will be coming at a time period defined by Joel as 'the day of the Lord.' It must be noted that these local judgments as in Joel are not types of 'the day the Lord' or a mini 'day of the Lord.' Joel makes this exceptionally clear.

> "Blow a trumpet in Zion, and sound an alarm on My holy mountain! Let all the inhabitants of the land tremble, <u>for the day of the LORD is coming;</u> surely it is near, A day of darkness and gloom, A day of clouds and thick darkness. As the dawn is spread over the mountains, *so* there is a great and mighty people; <u>there has never been *anything* like it, nor will there be again after it to the years of many generations</u>" (Joel 2:1-3).

There had been nothing like the future prophecy of 'the day of the Lord' when the Joel prophesy was presented to Israel. One cannot compare any local judgment, plague, disaster, etc. to the day of the Lord for nothing was like it or comparable. '<u>There has never been *anything* like it, nor will there be again after it to the years of many generations</u>' (2:8). Even the flood (Gen. 6-8) was nothing compared to the day of the Lord. One might even say the flood was just a little puddle compared to what is coming. The Joel warning concerning the day of the Lord should be extremely ominous to anyone reading this prophecy.

The day of the Lord is coming and there was nothing like it in the past, nothing comparable in the present, and

---

and Charles Augustus Briggs, *Enhanced Brown-Driver-Briggs Hebrew and English Lexicon*, electronic ed. (Oak Harbor, WA: Logos Research Systems, 2000), 572. To escape, to be delivered. Langenscheidt Hebrew Dictionary, Hodder and Stoughton, 180. The Lord will rescue or deliver those who call upon Him to do so during the day of the Lord. The context of this verse is exclusively that of the day of the Lord.

nothing like it again in the future. The day of the Lord or that day[5] has not happened yet. It will begin with His dreadful divine wrath on His entire creation. After that will be His future divine blessings in His kingdom reign for 1,000 years and then the eternal state (1 Cor. 15:24-25).[6]

Joel used this local plague as a warning

Joel used this locust disaster as a definite warning primarily to the nation Israel. Joel springboards into the future end time cataclysmic judgments. These are eschatological judgments which display the wrath of God (YHWH) known as the day of the Lord. It is most significant in defining the day of the Lord that this future time begins with His divine wrath and destruction.

> "Gird yourselves *with sackcloth*, and lament, O priests; Wail, O ministers of the altar! Come; spend the night in sackcloth, O ministers of my God, for the grain offering and the libation are withheld from the house of your God. Consecrate a fast, proclaim a solemn assembly; Gather the elders *and* all the inhabitants of the land to the house of the LORD your God, and cry out to the LORD. **Alas for the day! For the day of the LORD is near, And it will come as**

---

[5] It is noted that the day of the Lord is referenced at least 20 times in Zechariah as 'that day.'

[6] There will be more presented on this concerning the eternal state in the section on the kingdom. "Then *comes* the end, when He delivers up the kingdom to the God and Father, when He has abolished all rule and all authority and power. For He must reign until He has put all His enemies under His feet. The last enemy that will be abolished is death" (1 Cor. 15:24-26). He will deliver the kingdom back to the Father at the end of His earthly kingdom reign. So in a true sense the kingdom goes into the eternal state.

destruction[7] from the Almighty" (Joel 1:13-15).[8]

'And it will come as <u>destruction</u> from the Almighty' (3:15). The Hebrew word שֹׁד [9] means destruction, devastation,

---

[7] שֹׁד ...noun masc. **violence, havoc, devastation, ruin** ... *devastation, ruin*, for nation. Francis Brown, Samuel Rolles Driver and Charles Augustus Briggs, *Enhanced Brown-Driver-Briggs Hebrew and English Lexicon*, electronic ed. (Oak Harbor, WA: Logos Research Systems, 2000), 994.

[8] "The word of the LORD that came to Joel, the son of Pethuel. Hear this, O elders, And listen, all inhabitants of the land. Has *anything like* this happened in your days or in your fathers' days? Tell your sons about it, and *let* your sons *tell* their sons, and their sons the next generation. What the gnawing locust has left, the swarming locust has eaten; and what the swarming locust has left, the creeping locust has eaten; And what the creeping locust has left, the stripping locust has eaten. Awake, drunkards, and weep; And wail, all you wine drinkers, On account of the sweet wine That is cut off from your mouth. For a nation has invaded my land, mighty and without number; its teeth are the teeth of a lion, and it has the fangs of a lioness. It has made my vine a waste, and my fig tree splinters. It has stripped them bare and cast *them* away; their branches have become white. Wail like a virgin girded with sackcloth For the bridegroom of her youth. The grain offering and the libation are cut off from the house of the LORD. The priests mourn, the ministers of the LORD. The field is ruined, the land mourns, for the grain is ruined, The new wine dries up, Fresh oil fails. Be ashamed, O farmers, Wail, O vinedressers, for the wheat and the barley; Because the harvest of the field is destroyed. The vine dries up, and the fig tree fails; the pomegranate, the palm also, and the apple tree, All the trees of the field dry up. Indeed, rejoicing dries up from the sons of men. [13] Gird yourselves *with sackcloth*, And lament, O priests; Wail, O ministers of the altar! Come; spend the night in sackcloth, O ministers of my God, For the grain offering and the libation Are withheld from the house of your God" (Joel 1:1-13). <u>Joel springboards from this local locust disaster into the future end time judgments or eschatological judgments which begin the time period known as the day of the Lord. The day of the Lord will move from His divine wrath to the return of Christ and then His kingdom reign. There are some final judgments and then the eternal state.</u>

[9] שֹׁד ...noun masc. violence, havoc, devastation, ruin ... *devastation, ruin*, for nation. Francis Brown, Samuel Rolles Driver and Charles Augustus Briggs, *Enhanced Brown-Driver-Briggs Hebrew and English Lexicon*, electronic ed. (Oak Harbor, WA: Logos Research Systems, 2000), 994.

ruin, etc. and is from the root verb שָׁדַד [10] which has the ominous meaning of complete destruction or something violently destroyed.[11] Yet this complete looming destruction comes directly from the hand of the Almighty Himself. The locust plague points to something coming which is so devastating there is absolutely nothing comparable. Unger describes this localized judgment prefiguring a future devastation (Joel 1:1-13).

> "The locusts point to something still more terrible and form a prophetic picture of a greater disaster. They prefigure an invading army, 6–7 (cf. 2:25) and its desolation of the land. Both the vine (Ps 80:8, 14; Hos 10:1; Isa 5:1–7) and the fig tree symbolize Israel in her spiritual privilege and national election (Hos 9:10; Mt 24:32–33; Lk 13:67; Rom 11:17–24)… All people, 8–10, especially the farmer and vine growers, 11–12, the priests and all spiritual leaders of the nation, 13, are called to mourn."[12]

As Joel used this localized plague as a warning especially for Israel, the other Hebrew prophets will also use similar disasters as warnings of that terrifying day which is coming known as the day of the Lord. These warnings of a coming disaster are very consistent with the prophets, and all men should take heed concerning that terrifying coming day.

---

[10] שָׁדַד …vb. deal violently with, despoil, devastate, ruin …*violently destroy …be devastated*, of city …, country or nation[10] Francis Brown, Samuel Rolles Driver and Charles Augustus Briggs, *Enhanced Brown-Driver-Briggs Hebrew and English Lexicon*, electronic ed. (Oak Harbor, WA: Logos Research Systems, 2000), 994.

[11] Joel used this locust plague as a warning of the greatest time of divine devastation and destruction that was to come in His creation. This time period concerning the greatest future judgments is known as the day of the Lord or the day of YHWH or the day of Jehovah.

[12] Unger, M. F. (2005). *The new Unger's Bible handbook* (Rev. and updated ed.) (325). Chicago: Moody Publishers.

There seems to be very little interest today in taking the day of the Lord as major biblical doctrine. It appears the Thessalonians understood this day very well for Paul had taught them very well. This was perhaps the primary reason II Thessalonians was written. The Thessalonians thought they were in the day of the Lord (II Thess. 2:1-4). Paul made this very clear especially in II Thessalonians[13] that this was not possible. He had made this issue clear in 1 Thessalonians. What makes this so important is that no believer can possibly go into the day of the Lord. This is a huge issue especially for the church and this present church age.

The day of the Lord will eliminate all His enemies

The day of the Lord is coming and there has been nothing like it and there will be nothing like it ever again.[14] The day of the Lord judgments literally His

---

[13]The Thessalonians were terrified that the day of the Lord had come. Paul told them this was not possible until the apostasy comes first and the man of sin revealed. "Now we request you, brethren, with regard to the coming of our Lord Jesus Christ, and our gathering together to Him, that you may not be quickly shaken from your composure or be disturbed either by a spirit or a message or a letter as if from us, **to the effect that the day of the Lord has come**. Let no one in any way deceive you, **for *it will not come* unless the apostasy comes first, and the man of lawlessness is revealed, the son of destruction,** who opposes and exalts himself above every so-called god or object of worship, so that he takes his seat in the temple of God, displaying himself as being God" (2 Thes. 2:1-4). Yet Paul had instructed them as such in I Thessalonians for the rapture happens first (1 Thes. 4:13-18) and then the day of the Lord. "Now as to the times and the epochs, brethren, you have no need of anything to be written to you. For you yourselves know full well that the day of the Lord will come just like a thief in the night" (1 Thes. 5:1-2). Paul got much more technical in 2 Thessalonians concerning the day of the Lord and its timing. For more information see this author's book 'The Greatness of the Rapture.'

[14] The uniqueness of these forewarned judgments "Blow a trumpet in Zion, and sound an alarm on My holy mountain! Let all the inhabitants of the land tremble, For the day of the LORD is coming; Surely it is near, A day of darkness and gloom, A day of clouds and thick darkness. As the dawn is spread over the mountains, *so* there

divine fury and wrath dwarf any other judgment/s. This is why Joel was prophesying very clearly that no local plague, disaster, catastrophe, etc. is comparable to anything like that in the day of the Lord. Almost all the prophets warn Israel and the nations of this coming incomparable wrath. The forewarning is very clear especially to Israel that the day of the Lord is coming and all men should take this warning with the greatest admonition and fear. All this has been thoroughly established by most all the prophets of His Word and cannot be over emphasized!

This coming day begins the process of eliminating all His foes and enemies both in the heavens and on earth. In the angelic and human realms all rebellion and ungodliness will be eliminated prior to His kingdom. This will be a complete destruction of rebellion and a purging from the hand of the Almighty at His second coming. And then His kingdom will come. This will be the answer to the prayer of 'let Your kingdom come.'[15]

These judgments will include everything described by all the prophets concerning the day of the Lord with all the judgments of Revelation (Rev. 6-19).[16] These judgments build up in intensity as prophesied by

---

is a great and mighty people; **There has never been *anything* like it, Nor will there be again after it To the years of many generations**" (2:1-2).

[15]"Thy kingdom come. Thy will be done, On earth as it is in heaven" (Mat. 6:10); ἐλθέτω ἡ βασιλεία σου· γενηθήτω τὸ θέλημά σου, ὡς ἐν οὐρανῷ καὶ ἐπὶ γῆς· This is actually 'let Your kingdom come' as the verb ἐλθέτω is an aorist active imperative 3rd person singular and the emphasis is on the verb (come). Jesus taught His disciples to pray that the Lord bring in the/His covenanted kingdom. Lord 'bring in Your promised/covenanted kingdom. Many do not know they are praying for His kingdom to come. There is no covenanted kingdom at this time. His disciples should be prayer warriors for the coming kingdom.

[16]This will be all the judgments included in the seal, trumpet, and bowl judgments.

the seal, trumpet, and bowl judgments in Revelation. Even Christ described a great tribulation.[17] It must be noted that there is no kingdom covenanted or otherwise at this time during the church age. There is none in heaven other than His eternal reign and no covenanted kingdom has been established on the earth by Christ.[18] There must be a complete purging of His creation prior to His coming reign on the planet. Joel makes this very clear as well as all the other prophets. There is no kingdom until the complete purging of all evil, and can only be in the day of the Lord.

There will even be a second purging of all men at the beginning of His kingdom when He takes the covenanted throne of David. This is known as the sheep and goats judgment (Mat. 25:31-46).[19]   When Jesus takes His covenanted throne as Heir

---

[17]"For then there will be a great tribulation, such as has not occurred since the beginning of the world until now, nor ever shall" (Mat. 24:21). ἔσται γὰρ τότε θλῖψις μεγάλη οἵα οὐ γέγονεν ἀπ' ἀρχῆς κόσμου ἕως τοῦ νῦν οὐδ' οὐ μὴ γένηται. Christ defined a future time of 'great tribulation.' This is included in the day of the Lord and most likely toward the end where there an unprecedented climatic judgment. "Blow a trumpet in Zion, And sound an alarm on My holy mountain! Let all the inhabitants of the land tremble, For the day of the LORD is coming; Surely it is near, A day of darkness and gloom, A day of clouds and thick darkness. As the dawn is spread over the mountains, So there is a great and mighty people; There has never been anything like it, Nor will there be again after it To the years of many generations" (Joel 2:1-2). There is a direct correlation to the day of the Lord and 'great tribulation' defined by Christ. It must be noted that Christ was speaking also of His second coming and how it might be recognized. This is toward the end of the great judgments in the day of the Lord.

[18]This will be addressed in the section 'the times of the Gentiles.'
[19]"The words the nations (ta ethnē) should be translated "the Gentiles." These are all people, other than Jews, who have lived through the Tribulation period (cf. Joel 3:2, 12). They will be judged individually, not as national groups. They are described as a mingling of sheep and goats, which the Lord will separate... The King "on His throne" (v. 31) will extend an invitation to those on His right hand, the sheep, to enter the kingdom God had prepared ... since the Creation of the world. The basis of their

Apparent to the Davidic throne, He purges those who have made it through the last half of the 70th week of Daniel.[20] This time period of His wrath was defined by Christ as 'great tribulation' (Mat. 24:15-21). Toward the end of this time Christ will return, take His throne of His kingdom, and purge those who are left alive.

The day of the Lord begins as a time of His unprecedented wrath and no one will escape the fury of His judgments. As a note, this is why the Thessalonians were so fearful that they were in the 'day of the Lord.'[21] They fully

---

entrance is seen in their actions, for they provided food, **drink**, clothing, and care for the King (vv. 35–36). The King's statement will prompt the sheep to respond that they do not recall ever having ministered directly to the King (vv. 37–39). **The King will** answer that they performed these services for **the least of these brothers of Mine**, and by so doing were ministering to the King (v. 40). The expression "these brothers" must refer to a third group that is neither sheep nor goats. The only possible group would be Jews, physical brothers of the Lord. In view of the distress in the Tribulation period, it is clear that any believing Jew will have a difficult time surviving (cf. 24:15–21). The forces of the world dictator will be doing everything possible to exterminate all Jews (cf. Rev. 12:17). A Gentile going out of his way to assist a Jew in the Tribulation will mean that Gentile has become a believer in Jesus Christ during the Tribulation. By such a stand and action, a believing Gentile will put his life in jeopardy. His works will not save him; but his works will reveal that he is redeemed." Louis A. Barbieri and Jr., "Matthew" In , in *The Bible Knowledge Commentary: An Exposition of the Scriptures*, ed. J. F. Walvoord and R. B. Zuck (Wheaton, IL: Victor Books, 1985), Mt 25:31–40.

[20]This will be the judgment of the gentiles or nations concerning those who made it through the last 3.5 years of the 70th week of Daniel and lived. The sheep of this judgment are those who will enter the millennial kingdom.

[21] "Now we request you, brethren, with regard to the coming of our Lord Jesus Christ, and our gathering together to Him, that you may not be quickly shaken from your composure or be disturbed either by a spirit or a message or a letter as if from us, to the effect that the day of the Lord has come" (2 Thess. 2:1-2). There seemed to be rumors flying around Thessalonica that the day of the Lord has come. It has not and will not until certain things have taken place. This will be discussed further in a later section on the timing of the day of the Lord. For more information on the rapture of the church and the coming day of the Lord see this author's book titled 'The Greatness of the Rapture' and subtitled 'The Pre-Day of the Lord Rapture.'

understood this doctrine of His coming wrath as presented to them by Paul. They were taught that the rapture of the church must take place prior to the day of the Lord.

> "Now as to the times and the epochs, brethren, you have no need of anything to be written to you. For you yourselves know full well that <u>the day of the Lord </u>will come just like a thief in the night. While they are saying, Peace and safety! then destruction will come upon them suddenly like birth pangs upon a woman with child; and they shall not escape" (1Thess. 5:1-3).

The Thessalonians were terrified and were taught they had no part in the day of the Lord's wrath. They understood that would be raptured prior to this tremendous destruction of His coming wrath.

> "For they themselves report about us what kind of a reception we had with you, and how you turned to God from idols to serve a living and true God, and to wait for His Son from heaven, whom He raised from the dead, *that is* Jesus, who delivers us from the wrath to come" (1Thess. 1:9-10).

One hears very little of this today concerning a pre-day of the Lord rapture. The church cannot go into the day of the Lord especially as this begins with His coming wrath. The Scriptures are very clear on this teaching and extremely precise.

Joel's prophecy of coming devastation was a plea for repentance

Joel described this local locust plague in the land of Israel (1:1-1:12). Joel was calling for the repentance of the people of Israel especially the priests (1:13). He also called for all the people to cry out for His deliverance (1:14).

> "Gird yourselves *with sackcloth*, and lament, O priests; Wail, O ministers of the altar! Come; spend the night in sackcloth, O ministers of my God, for the grain offering and the libation are withheld from the house of your God.
> Consecrate a fast, Proclaim a solemn assembly; Gather the elders *and* all the inhabitants of the land to the house of the LORD your God, and cry out to the LORD" (Joe 1:13-14).

But then Joel forewarns all the people (Israel) of His coming judgments and wrath. He also describes much of what will happen in that day.

1) Alas for the day! For **the day of the LORD** is near (1:15a)
2) And it will come as destruction from the Almighty (1:15b)
3) Food, gladness and joy cut off (1:16)
4) Storehouses, barns, and grain destroyed (1:17)
5) No pasture for animals (1:18)
6) Fire has devoured all the pastures and trees (1:19)
7) The water brooks are dried up (1:20)
8) Blow a trumpet in Zion, Let all the inhabitants of the land tremble, for **the day of the LORD** is coming; Surely it is near (2:1)
9) A day of darkness and gloom, A day of clouds and thick darkness (2:2a)
10) There has never been *anything* like it, nor will there be again after it to the years of many generations (2:2b)

11) A fire consumes before them, and behind them a flame burns. The land is like the garden of Eden before them, but a desolate wilderness behind them, and nothing at all escapes them (2:3)

12) Their appearance is like the appearance of horses; and like war horses, so they run (2:4)

13) With a noise as of chariots they leap on the tops of the mountains, like the crackling of a flame of fire consuming the stubble, like a mighty people arranged for battle (2:5)

14) Before them the people are in anguish; all faces turn pale (2:6)

15) They run like mighty men; they climb the wall like soldiers; and they each march in line, nor do they deviate from their paths (2:7)

16) They do not crowd each other; they march everyone in his path. When they burst through the defenses, they do not break ranks (2:8)

17) They rush on the city, they run on the wall; they climb into the houses, they enter through the windows like a thief (2:9)

18) Before them the earth quakes, the heavens tremble, the sun and the moon grow dark, and the stars lose their brightness (2:10)

19) And the LORD utters His voice before His army; surely His camp is very great, for strong is he who carries out His word. **The day of the LORD** is indeed great and very awesome, and who can endure it? (2:11)

Note how the warnings of the day of the Lord are very clearly given by verses 1:15, 2:1, and 2:11. This appears to bring this section together linguistically and prophetically.

1) For the day of the LORD <u>is near</u> (1:15)
2) For the day of the LORD <u>is coming;
   surely it is near</u> (2:1)
3) The day of the LORD <u>is indeed great and
   very awesome, and who can endure it?</u>
   (2:11)

Joel is stating specific facts concerning the day of the
Lord. The day of the LORD is indeed great and exceedingly
awesome, and who can endure it? The answer is obviously no
one. Not one human, not one angel, or any creature will be able
to endure this time. So the prophet has moved from the local
locust plague to this future time of the day of the Lord with its
awesome ruin and complete devastation.

Many creatures have survived locust plagues and
various other plagues all over the world from time immemorial.
But no plague was ever called the day of the Lord with all the
details given by this prophecy in Joel especially 1:15-2:11.
There is obviously a weaving together of this plague with a
future time of His divine wrath and judgments. Yet these future
judgments have never happened as yet in any sense. After His
divine wrath has been poured out during the day of the Lord, it
will never be again as described in Joel and the other prophets.

This locust plague is a prophetic symbol or sign
exclusively for the warning concerning 'the day of the Lord.'
"Just as the Spirit of prophecy frequently uses some local
circumstance as the occasion of a far-reaching prophecy (cf. Isa
7:1–14 in the case of the virgin birth prediction) so the locust
plague is made a symbol of the yet-future Day of the Lord (Isa
2:12–22; 4:1–6; Ezk 30:3; Rev 19:11–21). In this apocalyptic
period (Rev 6–19) the Lord will manifest His power in putting
down His enemies actively and publicly in order to set up His
millennial kingdom over Israel. It is the period described
graphically in Ps 2."[22]

---

[22]Merrill Frederick Unger, *The New Unger's Bible Handbook*, Rev. and
updated ed. (Chicago: Moody Publishers, 2005), 325.

Major events in the day of the Lord

There is not enough space to describe all the events in the day of the Lord yet this is not very difficult. It is best to make a simple outline of certain events of this time period which are extremely significant. The following list or outline is just a brief overview of each section in Joel defining the day of the Lord.

This local judgment in Joel (1:1-14) begins the process of defining His coming wrath and blessings during the day of the Lord.

Local judgment – locust invasion (1:1-14)

<u>The day of the Lord</u> (1:15-3:21)

A future invasion (1:15-2:11)

A call for Israel's repentance (2:12-17)

A promise for His deliverance (2:18-27)

The pouring out of His Spirit on all flesh (2:28-32)

The restoration of Israel and judgments on nations (3:1-17)

His kingdom comes (3:18-21)

A future invasion (1:15-2:11)

This appears to be a future invasion which corresponds with Rev. 9:1-12. This may refer to the demon type locusts described in Revelation.[23] "And out of the smoke came forth

---

[23]"And the fifth angel sounded, and I saw a star from heaven which had fallen to the earth; and the key of the bottomless pit was given to him. And he opened the bottomless pit; and smoke went up out of the pit, like the smoke of a great furnace; and the sun and the air were darkened by the smoke of the pit. And out of the smoke came forth locusts upon the earth; and power was given them, as the scorpions of the earth have power. And they were told that they should not hurt the grass of the earth, nor any green thing, nor any tree, but only the men who do not have the seal of God on their foreheads. And they were not permitted to kill anyone, but to torment for five months; and their torment was like the torment of a scorpion when it stings a man. And in those days men will seek death and will not find it; and they will long to die and death flees from them. And the appearance of the

locusts upon the earth; and power was given them, as the scorpions of the earth have power. And they were told that they should not hurt the grass of the earth, nor any green thing, nor any tree, but only the men who do not have the seal of God on their foreheads" (Rev. 9:3-4).

This also may refer to the invasion of the king of the north (Ezek. 38:15-16; Dan. 11:40). For those who are present during the day of the Lord, they will know exactly what invasion this will be. No matter what is the exact nature of this specific invasion, this warning is grave, ominous, and deadly.

A call for Israel's repentance (2:12-17)

God calls for the repentance of national Israel. "Yet even now, declares the LORD, Return to Me with all your heart, and with fasting, weeping, and mourning; and rend your heart and not your garments. Now return to the LORD your God, for He is gracious and compassionate, slow to anger, abounding in lovingkindness, and relenting of evil" (Joel 2:12-13). The call for repentance is very solemn as God is calling His people to turn to Him (2:14-17). Why should they (the nations) say 'where is their God?'(17). "Let the priests, the LORD's ministers, weep between the porch and the altar, and let them say, spare Thy people, O LORD, And do not make Thine inheritance a reproach, A byword among the nations. Why should they among the peoples say, 'Where is their God?" (Joel 2:17). He will prove Himself to all the nations after He delivers Israel to their covenanted land and kingdom during the day of the Lord.

---

locusts was like horses prepared for battle; and on their heads, as it were, crowns like gold, and their faces were like the faces of men. And they had hair like the hair of women, and their teeth were like *the teeth* of lions. And they had breastplates like breastplates of iron; and the sound of their wings was like the sound of chariots, of many horses rushing to battle. And they have tails like scorpions, and stings; and in their tails is their power to hurt men for five months. They have as king over them, the angel of the abyss; his name in Hebrew is Abaddon, and in the Greek he has the name Apollyon. The first woe is past; behold, two woes are still coming after these things" (Rev. 9:1-12).

A promise for His deliverance (2:18-27)

God has promised His deliverance for Israel during the day of the Lord. He has great concern for His land and His people. He will have compassion on His covenant people and cause their future deliverance for His kingdom in the covenanted land of Israel. There is no Messianic covenanted kingdom outside His covenanted land. Abraham had one thing he was to see and that was the land. There is only one kingdom, and that kingdom will come during the day of the Lord. "Then the LORD will be zealous for His land, and will have pity on His people. And the LORD will answer and say to His people, Behold, I am going to send you grain, new wine, and oil, And you will be satisfied *in full* with them; And I will never again make you a reproach among the nations" (Joel 2:18-19).

The Lord will bless Israel in so many wonderful ways, and they will never again be put to shame or put out of His land. And the Lord will dwell among them as He has always promised[24] (20-27). "And you shall have plenty to eat and be satisfied, and praise the name of the LORD your God, Who has dealt wondrously with you; then My people will never be put to shame. Thus you will know that I am in the midst of Israel, and that I am the LORD your God and there is no other; and My people will never be put to shame" (Joel 2:26-27). Other writers and prophets also engage with these truths.

> "And I will dwell among the sons of Israel, and will not forsake My people Israel" (1 Kings 6:13); "And I will dwell among the sons of Israel

---

[24]"And He said to me, Son of man, *this is* the place of My throne and the place of the soles of My feet, where I will dwell among the sons of Israel forever. And the house of Israel will not again defile My holy name, neither they nor their kings, by their harlotry and by the corpses of their kings when they die" (Ezekiel 43:7). "And I will dwell among the sons of Israel and will be their God" (Ex. 29:45)
"And I will dwell among the sons of Israel, and will not forsake My people Israel" (1 Kings 6:13).

and will be their God" (Ex. 29:45); "And He said
to me, Son of man, *this is* the place of My throne
and the place of the soles of My feet, where I
will dwell among the sons of Israel forever. And
the house of Israel will not again defile My holy
name, neither they nor their kings, by their
harlotry and by the corpses of their kings when
they die" (Ezekiel 43:7).

There are so many other verses proving the redemption
of Israel and the Lord dwelling among His people. It must
constantly serve as a reminder that there is no covenanted
kingdom of God outside His covenanted land with His
covenanted people i.e. Israel. The church is never called Israel.
The church was never given a land and a king. There is no king
of the church. He is the Head and the Bridegroom to His body.
He is even the church's High Priest, but He was never called
King of His church.

The pouring out of His Spirit on all flesh (2:28-32)

During the day of the Lord, God will pour out His Spirit on
Israel. This has not happened yet in any manner for this will
not and cannot happen until the day the Lord. Peter was
quoting the Joel prophecy (Joel 2:28-32; Acts 2:17-21) which is
actually the entire chapter 3 of Joel from the Hebrew Text.

"And it will come about after this that I will pour
out My Spirit on all mankind; and your sons and
daughters will prophesy, Your old men will
dream dreams, Your young men will see visions.
And even on the male and female servants I will
pour out My Spirit in those days. And I will
display wonders in the sky and on the earth,
Blood, fire, and columns of smoke. The sun will
be turned into darkness, and the moon into
blood, before the great and awesome day of the
LORD comes. And it will come about that

whoever calls on the name of the LORD Will be delivered; For on Mount Zion and in Jerusalem There will be those who escape, As the LORD has said, Even among the survivors whom the LORD calls" (Joel 2:28-32 most English Texts; Joel 3 in the Hebrew Text; Joel 3 in the LXX; Acts 2:17-21)

When Peter quoted the Joel prophecy (Acts 2:28-32), he did not say this was happening on the day of Pentecost, for it was not. There was absolutely nothing happening from the Joel prophecy in any sense. The Joel prophecy will only be fulfilled in and during the day of the Lord. Also, Peter did not say 'this is that.' Peter said this is what the prophet Joel has said.[25] As Joel used a locust plague as the warning for the future day of the Lord, Peter is using this event of the Holy Spirit coming on the 12 apostles to show a greater and future pouring out of His Spirit. This future pouring out of His Spirit will be on 'all flesh' not just the 12 during the day of the Lord. It will be on the sons and daughters of Israel as well as all His servants. Absolutely none of this 'pouring out' has happened as yet.

> I.   And it will come about after this that I will pour out My Spirit on all mankind; and your sons and daughters will prophesy, Your old men will dream dreams, Your young men will see visions. And even on the male and female servants I will pour out My Spirit in those days.

---

[25] **"But this is what was spoken** of through the prophet Joel" Acts 2:16. ἀλλὰ τοῦτό ἐστιν τὸ εἰρημένον διὰ τοῦ προφήτου Ἰωήλ· Peter is just quoting what was spoken by Joel. He never said this was what was happening. He quoted Joel for this will only happen in the day of the Lord yet similar as when the Holy Spirit is poured out on all flesh.

II.   And I will display wonders in the sky and on the earth, Blood, fire, and columns of smoke.

III.   The sun will be turned into darkness,

IV.   and the moon into blood
        (*Note all the above has to happen before the climatic judgments of the day of the Lord*)

V.   <u>Before the great and awesome day of the LORD comes.</u>

It is very important to note that with the outpouring of His Spirit on all flesh (Israel in the day of the Lord), there will be accompanying great signs and wonders in the heavenlies. There were absolutely no accompanying signs in the heavenlies on the day of Pentecost especially with the coming of the Holy Spirit. It was to be on all flesh not just the 12. Also this has to happen before the climatic day of the Lord referring to the greater judgments during that future time period. This will be most likely towards the end of the 70th week of Daniel described by Christ as a great tribulation. Yet all this is included in the very great and awesome day of the Lord.

On the day of Pentecost this coming of the Holy Spirit was called Spirit baptism by Christ Himself. He is the Spirit Baptizer and this was fully confirmed to John. "And gathering them together, He commanded them not to leave Jerusalem, but to wait for what the Father had promised, "Which," *He said,* "you heard of from Me; for John baptized with water, but you shall be baptized with the Holy Spirit not many days from now" (Acts 1:4). Jesus did not relate 'you shall be baptized with the Holy Spirit' with anything connected with the Joel prophecy or with John's prophecies. This is very significant for if there were any connection to this prophecy, it is assumed Jesus would have made this very clear to the 12. Jesus did not do this and neither did Peter.

There is a simple conclusion that can be made from Joel 2:28-32 and Peter's message in Acts 2:22-36. During the day of the Lord and prior to His second coming, the Lord will pour out His Spirit on Israel (all flesh). There will also be all the accompanying signs in the heavenlies. Absolutely none of these things have happened as yet in any sense, for the day of the Lord has not yet come. This pouring out of the Spirit on Israel will only happen during the coming 'day of the Lord.' The day of the Lord had not started prior to Pentecost, neither on the day of Pentecost, or even until now.

Peter quoted the Joel prophecy

The main question would be why did Peter quote the Joel prophecy? When Peter addressed only the men of Israel[26] on the day of Pentecost, he was speaking to the same people who had witnessed the crucifixion of Jesus approximately 50 days earlier. Jesus had been confirmed to Israel with signs, miracles, and wonders (Acts 2:22-24). Israel as a nation had rejected the One Who is the Anointed to assume the covenanted throne of David. They had even rejected the forerunner and his message. What they were witnessing now on the day of Pentecost was the One Who was pouring out the Spirit (2:33). The One Who is the Spirit Baptizer.

There is a future time coming known as the day of the Lord when the Lord will pour out His Spirit on all Israel not just a few. This will also be a time of unprecedented annihilation and devastation. Absolutely none of this occurred on the day of Pentecost.

It must be thoroughly understood what Peter was doing. The Jewish crowds gathered and were watching what happened

---

[26]"Men of Israel, listen to these words: Jesus the Nazarene, a man attested to you by God with miracles and wonders and signs which God performed through Him in your midst, just as you yourselves know" (Acts 2:22). Peter was not addressing Gentiles or the church or anyone else but men of Israel. No Gentiles would be coming into the church until Acts 10 when Peter would be given special revelation about this (Acts 10). This may be as much as 5 or 10 years into the church age. Peter was amazed that Gentiles would be Spirit baptized the same way they were and he had to defend himself as such (Acts 11:15-18).

with these 12 disciples (Acts 2:5-13). Peter then presented a lengthy exhortation on the resurrection of Jesus (2:22-36). He then explained that these 12 apostles were not drunk (2:14-15), as then he quoted the Joel prophecy (2:17-21).

This was highly significant for a day is coming when the Holy Spirit would be poured out on all Israel not just a very few. Peter gave no indication that this was happening on the day of Pentecost. What was most important was this pouring out which Israel was witnessing first hand was being done by the resurrected and ascended Jesus Christ (2:30-36). He is the Spirit Baptizer doing what they were seeing and hearing. They were eye witnesses of the Spirit Baptizer's work.

> "This Jesus God raised up again, to which we are all witnesses. Therefore having been exalted to the right hand of God, and having received from the Father the promise of the Holy Spirit, **He has poured forth this which you both see and hear**. For it was not David who ascended into heaven, but he himself says: 'The Lord said to my Lord, Sit at My right hand, until I make Thine enemies a footstool for Thy feet. Therefore let all the house of Israel know for certain that God has made Him both Lord and Christ-- this Jesus whom you crucified" (Acts 2:32-33).

All the above especially 'He has poured forth this which you both see and hear' was demonstrative proof that Jesus had not only been resurrected, but He had also ascended and was exalted to the Father's right hand i.e. the place of divine preeminence. This proof goes way beyond Christ's own resurrection, for this confirms Him as both LORD and Christ eternally and by divine providence (Acts 2:22-24).[27]

---

[27]All this was divinely planned in eternity. "This *Man*, delivered up by the predetermined plan and foreknowledge of God, you nailed to a cross by the

Those who gathered on the day of Pentecost were all witnesses to this. He is the Lord, the eternal Son of God. He is also the Christ, the confirmed Anointed to assume the covenanted throne of David in Jerusalem over national Israel. This pouring out of the Spirit by Christ will happen prior to His ascending to His throne in Jerusalem.

As the High Priest, He was and is mediating the new covenant in the true tabernacle. However, He was never fulfilling any of the new covenant as this can only be fulfilled by Him with Israel in and during the day of the Lord. Peter never said anything about fulfillment of the Joel prophecy. There is absolutely no fulfilling of John's prophecies except the proof of Who the Spirit Baptizer is. Several facts were confirmed on the day of Pentecost and should have been obvious to all. Peter made this very simple and very clear.

Facts about Jesus confirmed on the day of Pentecost

1) Jesus *had* been resurrected (2:24-32)
2) Jesus *had* ascended (2:32-35)
3) Jesus *had* been exalted to the Father's throne (2:33)
4) **Jesus was the One pouring out the Spirit** (2:33)[28]

---

hands of godless men and put *Him* to death. And God raised Him up again, putting an end to the agony of death, since it was impossible for Him to be held in its power" (Act 2:23-24). All this was in the eternal plan of God. This was a true predestined plan designed by the True Predestinator. τοῦτον τῇ ὡρισμένῃ βουλῇ καὶ προγνώσει τοῦ θεοῦ ἔκδοτον διὰ χειρὸς ἀνόμων προσπήξαντες ἀνείλατε (2:23). Yet He Himself created the ages "By faith we understand that the worlds (ages) were prepared by the word of God, so that what is seen was not made out of things which are visible" (Heb 11:3). It was all planned by Him.

[28]John confirms Jesus as the One Who baptizes in the Holy Spirit. Jesus is confirmed as the Holy Spirit Baptizer. "And I did not recognize Him, but He who sent me to baptize in water said to me, 'He upon whom you see the Spirit descending and remaining upon Him, this is the one who baptizes in the Holy Spirit" (John 1:33).

5) Jesus is confirmed LORD=Eternal Son (2:36)
6) Jesus is confirmed Messiah (2:36)
7) This was the same Jesus Who had been crucified (2:22-23)
8) **Jesus will pour out the Spirit in the day of the Lord** (2:17-21)[29]

Again, what is so essential is that all the Jews who were present on the day of Pentecost were witnesses to a pouring out of the Holy Spirit on the 12 apostles. "Therefore having been exalted to the right hand of God, and having received from the Father the promise of the Holy Spirit, He has poured forth this which you both see and hear" (Act 2:33). This pouring out of the Spirit is Spirit Baptism. This Spirit baptism places the believers into the body of Christ. "For by one Spirit we were all baptized into one body, whether Jews or Greeks, whether slaves or free, and we were all made to drink of one Spirit" (1 Cor.12:13). This body is His church which He is building at the present time from the day of Pentecost. "And I also say to you that you are Peter, and upon this rock I will build My church; and the gates of Hades shall not overpower it" (Mat 16:18). Jesus is not building Israel, He is building His church.

His church or body is defined by Spirit baptism which He performs as He did on the day of Pentecost. This Spirit baptism will end at the rapture of the church for the church is then complete. Then at the rapture, all the church will meet Him in the air. He, the Spirit Baptizer, meets His body the church at this glorious event. This glorious event began on the day of Pentecost and will end on the glorious day of the rapture.

Joel's prophecy was that of gloom, doom, and destruction for it only occurs in the day of the Lord. The day of Pentecost and Joel's prophesy are two completely separate events, time periods, separated by two different Spirit baptisms or Spirit outpourings. The pouring out of the Holy Spirit on the

---

[29]See previous footnote.

day of Pentecost was a glorious event which was not prophesied by Joel. The pouring out of the Holy Spirit on the day of Pentecost was prophesied by Jesus.

The restoration of Israel and judgments on nations (3:1-17)

Intermixed with judgments in the day of the Lord are the promises of restoration for Israel as His covenanted people in the earthly kingdom.

> "For behold, in those days and at that time, when I restore the fortunes of Judah and Jerusalem, I will gather all the nations, and bring them down to the valley of Jehoshaphat. Then I will enter into judgment with them there On behalf of My people and My inheritance, Israel, Whom they have scattered among the nations; And they have divided up My land. They have also cast lots for My people, Traded a boy for a harlot, And sold a girl for wine that they may drink" (Joe 3:1-3).

These nations are being judged primarily for their treatment of God's covenanted people which is national Israel.[30] All this stems from the unilateral, eternal, and unconditional Abrahamic covenant. "And I will bless those who bless you, and the one who curses you I will curse. And in you all the families of the earth shall be blessed" (Gen 12:3).

> "In those days and at that time' denotes that phase of the Day of the Lord which will witness Israel's restoration (Isa 11:10–12; Jer 23:5–8; Ezk 37:21–28; Acts 15:15–17). This passage is introductory to the primary theme of the judgment of the nations, 2–8, inasmuch as that

---

[30]The church as His body is not a covenanted people as is Israel. There are no covenants with the church although they celebrate many blessings from the eternal covenants.

event is a necessary prerequisite to Israel's reinstatement. The nations that have persecuted Israel must be judged before Israel can be brought into safety and blessing (cf. Mt 25:31–46; Rom 11:25–27; Zech 6:1–8; Rev 16:14). 2–16. The nations judged. The Lord Himself is the speaker, 2–8. He announces what He will do to Israel's enemies when He restores His people (note 'my people,' 3). The place of the judgment is said to be 'the Valley of Jehoshaphat,' 2, 12. This is usually taken as a symbolic rather than a geographical name, as inferred from the etymology, '*Yahweh* shall judge' and from 14, where the same valley is called the 'valley of decision,' in the sense of a judicial sentence or verdict (rendered against the wicked nations judged there). However, both Joel and Zechariah (cf. Zech 14:4) evidently regarded this theater of judgment as the Kidron Valley and the widening mountain basin to the south of the city beyond Hinnom. Kidron is now also known as the valley of Jehoshaphat, called so as early as Eusebius, but evidently on the basis of the Joel and Zechariah passages. The basis of the judgment will be 'concerning my inheritance, my people Israel."[31]

The judgment of these nations is real and only happens in the day of the Lord. As there are other judgments for the treatment of Israel, God's covenanted people, the judgments in Joel are only in the day of the Lord.

---

[31]Merrill Frederick Unger, *The New Unger's Bible Handbook*, Rev. and updated ed. (Chicago: Moody Publishers, 2005), 326.

His kingdom comes (3:18-21)

His kingdom finally comes with His kingdom blessings especially for Israel yet only after the time of His judgments and wrath in the day of the Lord.

Israel will never have a lack of respect from any people or nation again. "And the LORD will answer and say to His people, behold, I am going to send you grain, new wine, and oil, and you will be satisfied *in full* with them; And I will never again make you a reproach among the nations" (2:19).

The Lord will restore national Israel to His covenanted land especially Judah and Jerusalem. All the nations will know this for a fact that the Lord dwells in Zion during the kingdom. "Then you will know that I am the LORD your God, dwelling in Zion My holy mountain. So Jerusalem will be holy, and strangers will pass through it no more" (Joel 3:17). In the kingdom the Lord will dwell with His people in the land. And Judah will be inhabited forever. All this will go into eternity when the kingdom is transferred to the eternal state.[32] "But Judah will be inhabited forever, And Jerusalem for all generations. And I will avenge their blood which I have not avenged, For the LORD dwells in Zion" (Joel 3:20-21). This will be discussed further in the section on "Christ's Kingdom."

Conclusion

The day of the Lord is major doctrine. Joel is the first prophet who mentions the day of the Lord. Joel definitively includes the following in the day of the Lord. As some of the issues may be interwoven as to order or timing, it is very clear what the day of the Lord includes:

---

[32]"Then *comes* the end, when He delivers up the kingdom to the God and Father, when He has abolished all rule and all authority and power. For He must reign until He has put all His enemies under His feet" (1 Cor. 15:24-25).

1) Destruction from God the Almighty (Joel 1:15)
2) All the judgments described by Joel (Joel 1:1-3:17)
3) The pouring out of the Holy Spirit on all flesh i.e. *Israel* (2:28)
4) Climatic final phase of the great and terrible day of the Lord (2:32)
5) The gathering of all nations for judgment (3:2)
6) His future kingdom reign and blessings (3:17-21)
7) Judah and Jerusalem will be inhabited forever (3:20)[33]
8) The Lord will avenge *all* the enemies of Israel (3:21)
9) The Lord will literally dwell in literal Zion (3:21)[34]

So in defining the day of the Lord at least from the prophet Joel, all the above must be included in explaining the day of the Lord. The day of the Lord is major biblical doctrine which begins with His wrath and ends with His kingdom and His kingdom blessings. The kingdom is transferred into the eternal state (1 Cor. 15:24-25; 2 Peter 3:10-14).

---

[33]See previous footnote.

[34] In the kingdom the Lord will dwell among His people Israel. This is very significant. "And the Spirit lifted me up and brought me into the inner court; and behold, the glory of the LORD filled the house. [6] Then I heard one speaking to me from the house, while a man was standing beside me. [7] And He said to me, "Son of man, *this is* the place of My throne and the place of the soles of My feet, where I will dwell among the sons of Israel forever. And the house of Israel will not again defile My holy name, neither they nor their kings, by their harlotry and by the corpses of their kings when they die" (Ezekiel 43:5-7).

Chapter 3
The day of the Lord in Obadiah

Obadiah and his warning to the nations

Obadiah was written to the northern kingdom of Israel. As Joel was the first of the writing prophets to the southern kingdom of Judah, Obadiah may have been the first of the writing prophets to the northern kingdom of Israel.[1] No matter what the dating or the audience, his message is very clear and powerful. The dating of Obadiah appears to coincide with the reign of Jehoram (853-841 B.C.).[2]

Obadiah is the shortest book in the Hebrew Text. Yet this book is as potent as any prophecy in the Text. Obadiah predicted not only the complete destruction of Edom and other nations, but the precise reason for their total destruction and devastation. The nature of the destruction of Edom and the others nations is so powerful that the prophet said they will be as if they never existed. This can be gleaned easily from the prophecy made to Edom. "Because just as you drank on My holy mountain, all the nations will drink continually. They will drink and swallow, and become as if they had never existed" (Oba. 1:16).

---

[1] Obadiah directly addresses Edom and the other nations and their treatment of Israel and Jerusalem.

[2] Although numerous critics deny the unity of the prophecy, placing it in the Chaldean period after Jerusalem's fall in 586 B.C. or later, it is best to hold to the authenticity of the book and date it during the reign of Jehoram (c. 853–841 B.C.). At that time the Philistines and Arabians invaded Judah and plundered Jerusalem (2 Chr 21:16–17; Joel 3:3–6; Amos 1:6). The Edomites were also bitter enemies of Judah in that period (2 Kgs 8:20–22; 2 Chr 21:8–10). Thus, the requirements of Obadiah's having written this prophecy are satisfied in the historical context… Amos (c. 760 B.C.) shows acquaintance with Obadiah (cf. 4 with Amos 9:2; vv. 9, 10, 18 with Amos 1:11–12; v. 14 with Amos 1:6, 9; v. 19 with Amos 9:14). Jeremiah apparently used this prophecy also (cf. Jer 49:7–22 with Ob 1–6). This gives additional support for an early date for the prophecy. Merrill Frederick Unger, *The New Unger's Bible Handbook*, Rev. and updated ed. (Chicago: Moody Publishers, 2005), 332.

As Joel used a local plague to warn of a pending doom in the day of the Lord, Obadiah used the prophesied destruction of Edom as a warning for the coming day of the Lord. "This is the shortest prophecy and the smallest book of the OT. Its author was Obadiah, whose name means 'the servant of the Lord.' The prophecy is wholly taken up with the condemnation of Edom for its treachery toward Judah, with a prophecy of its utter destruction and Judah's salvation in the Day of the Lord."[3]

Obadiah deals directly with Edom

Obadiah received a vision from the Lord God concerning the land and people of Edom. The Edomites were the direct descendants of Esau, Jacob's twin brother. The Edomites were in constant conflict and avid enemies with Israel the descendants of Jacob.

This vision given to Obadiah by the Lord God begins with a condemning message to Edom. The Lord relates in just a few words how despised Edom is to Him.

"The vision of Obadiah. <u>Thus says the Lord God concerning Edom</u>-- We have heard a report from the LORD, and an envoy has been sent among the nations saying, Arise and let us go against her for battle
1. <u>Behold, I will make you small among the nations;</u>
2. <u>You are greatly despised.</u>
3. <u>The arrogance of your heart has deceived you,</u>
4. You who live in the clefts of the rock, in the loftiness of your dwelling place, <u>who say in your heart, 'Who will bring me down to earth?</u>

[3]Merrill Frederick Unger, *The New Unger's Bible Handbook*, Rev. and updated ed. (Chicago: Moody Publishers, 2005), 332.

5. Though you build high like the eagle, though
   you set your nest among the stars, <u>from there
   I will bring you down</u>," declares the LORD.
   (Oba. 1:1-4).

There will be a complete destruction of Edom.
"Obadiah, sensing the intensity of God's judgment on Esau's
descendants, then stated the reasons for God's condemnation.
The prophet spoke of the Edomites' sinful attitudes (vv. 10–12)
and their actions against Judah (vv. 13–14)."[4]

1. "<u>Because of violence to your brother Jacob,</u>
2. You will be covered *with* shame, and you will be cut off
   forever.
3. <u>On the day that you stood aloof, on the day that
   strangers carried off his wealth, and foreigners entered
   his gate and cast lots for Jerusalem-- You too were as
   one of them.</u>
4. <u>Do not gloat over your brother's day, the day of his
   misfortune.</u>
5. And <u>do not rejoice over the sons of Judah In the day of
   their destruction</u>; yes, do not boast in the day of *their*
   distress. Do not enter the gate of My people In the day
   of their disaster.
6. Yes, you, <u>do not gloat over their calamity in the day of
   their disaster.</u>
7. And <u>do not loot their wealth in the day of their disaster.</u>
8. And <u>do not stand at the fork of the road to cut down
   their fugitives;</u>
9. And <u>do not imprison their survivors In the day of their
   distress</u>" (Oba. 1:10-14).

---

[4]Walter L. Baker, "Obadiah" In , in *The Bible Knowledge Commentary: An
Exposition of the Scriptures*, ed. J. F. Walvoord and R. B. Zuck (Wheaton,
IL: Victor Books, 1985), Ob 10–14.

Edom had committed many offences to the Lord and the list goes on and on. The greatest seems to be pride and all the injustice done against their brother Jacob (1:10). This is also a warning to all nations in how they treat Israel. Even though Edom will be destroyed, Obadiah used this judgment to warn all the nations that the day of the Lord was coming.

The day of the Lord in Obadiah

As judgment will come upon Edom, so it will come on all nations in the day of the Lord. .

- "For the day of the LORD draws near on all the nations. As you have done, it will be done to you. Your dealings will return on your own head" (Oba. 1:15).

The Edomites were being judged on how they treated their brother Jacob. This was also a warning to the nations that the day of the Lord is coming and they would be judged in a similar way as Edom. "In verse 15 the prophet links the future with the past in a prediction still unfulfilled, 'The Day of the Lord is near for all nations.' All nations will be judged as to their treatment of Israel, as Edom was (cf. Mt 25:31–46; Rev 16:13–16; with Joel 3:1–14). Jacob's deliverance and salvation, 17–20, are described (cf. Joel 2:32)."[5]

Kingdom blessings in the day of the Lord

Yet there will also be blessings in the day of the Lord, for Obadiah speaks of the coming kingdom.

- "But on Mount Zion there will be those who escape, and it will be holy. And the house of Jacob will possess their possessions" (Oba. 1:17).[6]

---

[5]Merrill Frederick Unger, *The New Unger's Bible Handbook*, Rev. and updated ed. (Chicago: Moody Publishers, 2005), 333.

[6]"Though Esau will be destroyed by God's wrath, Israel in God's grace will experience **deliverance**. Israel will be freed from her enemies. **Mount Zion** (cf. v. 21), a synonym for Jerusalem… though desecrated by Edom (Obad.

- "The deliverers will ascend Mount Zion to judge the mountain of Esau, and the kingdom will be the LORD's" (Oba. 1:21).

It is very consistent with the prophets to move from a local judgment to the future day of the Lord. The day of the Lord begins with His wrath and then comes the blessings of His covenanted kingdom. "From Jerusalem (Mount Zion; cf. v. 17) deliverers (judges) will ... govern the people who will have occupied the mountains of Esau (cf. vv. 8, 19). In the Millennium, the kingdom will belong to the Lord (cf. Zech. 14:9). Israel will be restored as a nation (Obad. 17), she will occupy the land (vv. 18–20), and she will be ruled by her King, the Lord Himself (v. 21)."[7]

Conclusion

Obadiah presents a very powerful message. The warning to Edom (the Edomites) was very clear. They were very prideful and arrogant who had no fear of God but had a complete disregard for His covenant people, Israel. There were blessings and cursings which have followed Israel beginning

---

13), **will be holy** (cf. Isa. 52:1; Zech. 14:20–21), and the land promised to Israel (Gen. 15:18–21) will be occupied by **the house** (descendants) **of Jacob** (cf. Obad. 19–20). God's covenant people who trust Him will finally be delivered; they will be set apart to God. **Jacob** (the Southern Kingdom) and **Joseph** (the Northern Kingdom) will be united (cf. Ezek. 37:15–23), and will destroy Edom (**the house of Esau;** cf. Obad. 6) like **a flame** easily setting **stubble ... on fire** (cf. Zech. 12:6; Mal. 4:1). Then the Edomites, Israel's longtime enemies, will finally be wiped out. Edom **will** have **no survivors,** in reprisal for her treatment of Judah's survivors (Obad. 14). The certainty of this truth is affirmed by the words, **The LORD has spoken.** Since He has said it, none should question it" Walter L. Baker, "Obadiah" In , in *The Bible Knowledge Commentary: An Exposition of the Scriptures*, ed. J. F. Walvoord and R. B. Zuck (Wheaton, IL: Victor Books, 1985), Ob 17–20.

[7] Walter L. Baker, "Obadiah" In , in *The Bible Knowledge Commentary: An Exposition of the Scriptures*, ed. J. F. Walvoord and R. B. Zuck (Wheaton, IL: Victor Books, 1985), Ob 21.

with their forefather Abraham. "And I will bless those who bless you, and the one who curses you I will curse. And in you all the families of the earth shall be blessed" (Gen. 12:3). 'Because of the violence done to your brother Jacob' (Oba. 1:15), Edom would be completely cut off or destroyed. The warning went out to all the nations to listen to the Word of the Lord, for the day of the Lord is coming. No one will escape who has not turned to the Lord and believe His Word.

Chapter 4
The day of the Lord in Zephaniah

The book of Zephaniah reveals many ominous judgments which are coming during the future day of the Lord. Zephaniah uses the term 'the day of the Lord' more than any other prophet. He concentrates primarily on the severity of the judgments in the day of the Lord.

As Joel and Obadiah warned of the future day of Lord by using some local incident as a warning, Zephaniah does exactly the same. The immediate pending judgment on Judah, the southern kingdom, was for continued idolatry and simply turning from the Lord (Zeph. 1:4-6).[1] Zephaniah used this warning and judgment on Judah as a forewarning of the coming day of the Lord.

The judgments in the day of the Lord are those of the future wrath of God for the purging of a God rejecting world. Zephaniah makes this extremely graphic.

A warning of universal judgment

God spoke His word by the prophet Zephaniah to Judah, and judgment was the theme of his message. Zephaniah begins with a coming universal judgment which will come in the day of the Lord.[2] Zephaniah 1:1-3 speaks of the "judgment of the whole earth. Zephaniah ('the Lord hides or protects') was perhaps a great grandson of Hezekiah. The scope of these verses embraces a worldwide judgment of the Day of the Lord

---

[1]The immediate warnings that were given to Judah, the southern kingdom, concerned their idolatrous departure from their covenant keeping Lord. This is significant as the day of the Lord judgments were woven into his message.
[2]"The message of Zephaniah begins with a universal judgment (see Gen. 6-8). These words not only introduce the particular judgment that would be pronounced upon Judah (v. 4), but they also speak of the final judgment that will usher in the kingdom of God on earth." Earl D. Radmacher, gen. ed., *The Nelson Study Bible* (Nashville: Thomas Nelson, 1997), 1526.

(cf.1:17; 2:11, 14, 15)."[3] Observe the severity of these future universal judgments.

- "The word of the LORD which came to Zephaniah son of Cushi, son of Gedaliah, son of Amariah, son of Hezekiah, in the days of Josiah[4] son of Amon,
- I will completely remove all *things* from the face of the earth," declares the LORD.
- I will remove man and beast;
- I will remove the birds of the sky And the fish of the sea, And the ruins along with the wicked;
- And I will cut off man from the face of the earth, declares the LORD" (Zech. 1:1-3).

These judgments are universal and involve even the animal world. By presenting this format of universal judgments first, the emphasis of Zephaniah is on the day of the Lord. The warning is just that, the day of the Lord is coming and it will be a complete removal or purging of all living creatures.

Local judgment of Judah and Jerusalem

The prophet moves from these future judgments during the day of the Lord to the local judgment/s of Judah and Jerusalem[5] resulting from their continued idolatry (1:4-6). "The Lord will destroy Judah's ungodly religious syncretism. Molech, vs 5, was the chief Ammonite deity. [6] The Assyrians

---

[3]Merrill Frederick Unger, *The New Unger's Bible Handbook*, Rev. and updated ed. (Chicago: Moody Publishers, 2005), 345.
[4]The reign of Josiah over the southern kingdom is dated about 640-609 B.C.
[5]This refers to the southern kingdom.
[6]Milcom or Molech, an Ammonite deity worshiped by human sacrifice; "And they built the high places of Baal that are in the valley of Ben-hinnom to cause their sons and their daughters to pass through *the fire* to Molech, which I had not commanded them nor had it entered My mind that they should do this abomination, to cause Judah to sin" (Jer. 32:35).

adored 'the starry host.'" [7] Note how the prophet singles out Judah and Jerusalem and their specific transgressions.

- "So I will stretch out My hand <u>against Judah and against all the inhabitants of Jerusalem</u>.
- And <u>I will cut off the remnant of Baal</u> from this place, *And* the names of the <u>idolatrous priests along with the priests</u>.
- And those who <u>bow down on the housetops to the host of heaven</u>, And those who bow down *and* swear to the LORD and <u>*yet* swear by Milcom</u>,
- And those <u>who have turned back from following the LORD</u>,
- And those <u>who have not sought the LORD or inquired of Him</u>" (Zeph. 1:4-6).

Note all the idolatry that was charged against the southern kingdom.   They could swear equally to the Lord and at the same time to Milcom.   It appears even the entire priesthood had turned to idolatry and had become completely idolatrous.

- Baal worship
- idolatrous priests
- those who bow down on the housetops to the host of heaven
- those who bow down *and* swear to Milcom
- those who have turned back from LORD
- those who have not sought the LORD or inquired of Him

There was a pending judgment for their wickedness which would come when Babylon under Nebuchadnezzar took

---

[7] Merrill Frederick Unger, *The New Unger's Bible Handbook*, Rev. and updated ed. (Chicago: Moody Publishers, 2005), 345.

the southern kingdom into captivity. "The imminent invasion of the Chaldeans under Nebuchadnezzar is treated as a prefigurement of the apocalyptic Day of the Lord in which all earth judgments culminate (cf. Isa 2: 10–22; Joel 1–2; Rev 19:11–21)."[8]

As the Babylonian captivity was very literal so is the warning of the future day of the Lord for Israel as well as the entire world. The Lord is warning the world of a future day of His wrath which is known biblically as the day of the Lord. He will judge and purge the world and bring in His kingdom. He will set His King, the Lord Jesus Christ on His throne[9] over Israel.

The day of the Lord in Zephaniah

Zephaniah uses the term 'the day of the Lord' seven times. As there are other references to this coming day, Zephaniah's central message is judgment and he certainly gives much information about this dreadful time coming upon the planet and all mankind.

1) "Be silent before the Lord God! For <u>the day of the LORD</u> is near, For the LORD has prepared a sacrifice, He has consecrated His guests" (Zephaniah 1:7).
2) "Then it will come about on <u>the day of the LORD</u>'s sacrifice, That I will punish the princes, the king's sons, and all who clothe themselves with foreign garments" (Zephaniah 1:8).

---

[8]Ibid., p. 345.
[9]"The Lord adopts the covenanted kingdom and throne over Israel as His own. "But I will settle him <u>in My house and in My kingdom forever,</u> and his throne shall be established forever" (1Chron. 17:14); "And of all my sons (for the LORD has given me many sons), He has chosen my son Solomon to sit on the throne of the kingdom of the LORD over Israel" (1 Chron. 28:5).

3) "Near is <u>the great day of the LORD</u>, near and coming very quickly; listen, <u>the day of the LORD</u>! In it the warrior cries out bitterly" (Zephaniah 1:14).[10]

4) "Neither their silver nor their gold Will be able to deliver them On <u>the day of the LORD</u>'s wrath; And all the earth will be devoured In the fire of His jealousy, For He will make a complete end, Indeed a terrifying one, Of all the inhabitants of the earth" (Zephaniah 1:18).

5) "Before the decree takes effect-- The day passes like the chaff-- Before the burning anger of the LORD comes upon you, Before <u>the day of the LORD</u>'s anger comes upon you" (Zephaniah 2:2).

---

[10]Note all the details of Zeph. 1:14-18 concerning the day of the Lord. Zephaniah goes into many details and the list just seems to go on and on. The warning is out about the future day of the Lord. I t is truly pending doom on the planet and on all men.

1. "Near is the great day of the LORD, near and coming very quickly; listen, the day of the LORD!
2. In it the warrior cries out bitterly.
3. A day of wrath is that day,
4. A day of trouble and distress,
5. A day of destruction and desolation,
6. A day of darkness and gloom
7. A day of clouds and thick darkness
8. A day of trumpet and battle cry, against the fortified cities and the high corner towers
9. And I will bring distress on men, So that they will walk like the blind, Because they have sinned against the LORD;
10. And their blood will be poured out like dust, And their flesh like dung.
11. Neither their silver nor their gold Will be able to deliver them On the day of the LORD's wrath;
12. And all the earth will be devoured In the fire of His jealousy,
13. For He will make a complete end, Indeed a terrifying one, Of all the inhabitants of the earth" (Zeph. 1:14-18).

6) "Seek the LORD, All you humble of the earth who have carried out His ordinances; Seek righteousness, seek humility. Perhaps you will be hidden In <u>the day of the LORD</u>'s anger" (Zephaniah 2:3).

There is a tremendous amount of information presented in all Zephaniah's references to the day of the Lord.   Just from the immediate references, all this can be gleaned.

- "Be silent before the Lord God! For the day of the LORD is near, <u>For the LORD has prepared a sacrifice, He has consecrated His guests</u>" (Zephaniah 1:7).

- "Then it will come about on the day of the LORD's sacrifice, That <u>I will punish the princes, the king's sons, and all who clothe themselves with foreign garments</u>" (Zephaniah 1:8).

- "Near is the great day of the LORD, near and coming very quickly; listen, the day of the LORD! <u>In it the warrior cries out bitterly</u>" (Zephaniah 1:14).

- "Neither their silver nor their gold Will be able to deliver them On the day of the LORD's wrath; <u>And all the earth will be devoured In the fire of His jealousy, For He will make a complete end, Indeed a terrifying one, Of all the inhabitants of the earth</u>" (Zephaniah 1:18).

- "Before the decree takes effect-- The day passes like the chaff-- <u>Before the burning anger of the LORD comes upon you</u>, Before the day of the LORD's <u>anger comes upon you</u>" (Zephaniah 2:2).

- "Seek the LORD, All you humble of the earth who have carried out His ordinances; Seek righteousness, seek humility. Perhaps you will be hidden in the day of the LORD's anger" (Zephaniah 2:3).

What can be easily observed from these verses are the terrifying events that will occur during the day of the Lord. If the warnings of judgment were real concerning Judah's idolatry resulting in the Babylon captivity, then the judgments of the day of the Lord are certainly just as real.

Again, God uses this specific warning and judgment of Judah as a future warning of the day of the Lord. But the judgments of the day of the Lord are completely incomparable. He says that He will make a clean sweep of this entire planet in which everything will be judged, and there will be a complete end. Observe the judgments listed especially those associated with the day of the Lord in context.

- The LORD has prepared a sacrifice
- I will punish the princes
- The warrior cries out bitterly
- All the earth will be devoured
- He will make a complete and terrifying end of all earth's inhabitants
- The burning anger of the LORD
- The LORD's anger

The Lord warns all the nations of the pending doom and catastrophic judgments during the day of the Lord. No nation and no one will escape His judgments.

1. "Therefore, wait for Me, declares the LORD, for the day when I rise up to the prey.
2. Indeed, My decision is to gather nations,
3. to assemble kingdoms,
4. to pour out on them My indignation,

5. all My burning anger;
6. For all the earth will be devoured by the fire of My zeal"
    (Zeph. 3:8).

And Zephaniah presented many more related judgments
to the above in the day of the Lord, yet he implores Judah as
well as all men to humbly seek the Lord and His righteousness.
All men need His righteousness, for all men are unrighteous.

1. "Gather yourselves together, yes, gather, O nation
    without shame, before the decree takes effect-- The day
    passes like the chaff—
2. Before the burning anger of the LORD comes upon you,
3. Before the day of the LORD's anger comes upon you.
4. Seek the LORD, All you humble of the earth who have
    carried out His ordinances; seek righteousness, seek
    humility.
5. Perhaps you will be hidden in the day of the LORD's
    anger" (Zeph. 2:1-3).

The Lord's anger that is His wrath[11] is what is coming
on a God rejecting world. All men not only reject their Creator
but don't want their true Creator in any sense. They reject
everything about Him and all He has lovingly done for them.
Yet He reaches out to all men especially having given His
Son.[12] He implores all to turn to Him with humility before it is
too late. One day it will be too late. Almost all the prophets
warned of the coming day of the Lord and His wrath.
Zephaniah's primary message is judgment that is coming in the
day of the Lord. He pleads that all men would turn to Him.

---

[11]"Who can stand before His indignation? Who can endure the burning of
His anger? His wrath is poured out like fire, and the rocks are broken up by
Him" (Nah. 1:6)/
[12]"But God demonstrates His own love toward us, in that while we were yet
sinners, Christ died for us" (Rom. 5:8).

Kingdom blessings in the day of the Lord

After His wrath of the day of the Lord, there follows the covenanted kingdom blessings. There are many future blessings for the Gentiles. The covenanted kingdom blessings are sometimes woven into the actually judgment verses of His coming wrath.

Judgment of the nations was pronounced in Zeph.3:8. Then after the judgments of that day comes the blessings of His kingdom. "For then I will give to the peoples purified lips, that all of them may call on the name of the LORD, to serve Him shoulder to shoulder. From beyond the rivers of Ethiopia My worshipers, My dispersed ones, Will bring My offerings" (Zeph. 3:9-10).

But He must first restore Israel especially Jerusalem. This will be after His wrath in the day of the Lord. Only when the kingdom is restored will the King be in the midst of Israel. There is no kingdom without His Personal presence as *the* King.

1. Shout for joy, O daughter of Zion! Shout *in triumph*, O Israel! Rejoice and exult with all *your* heart, O daughter of Jerusalem!

2. The LORD has taken away *His* judgments against you, He has cleared away your enemies.

3. The King of Israel, the LORD, is in your midst; you will fear disaster no more.

4. In that day it will be said to Jerusalem: "Do not be afraid, O Zion; do not let your hands fall limp. The LORD your God is in your midst, a victorious warrior. He will exult over you with joy, He will be quiet in His love, He will rejoice over you with shouts of joy.

5. I will gather those who grieve about the appointed feasts-- They came from you, *O Zion; The* reproach *of exile* is a burden on them. Behold, I am going to deal at that time With all your oppressors,

6. I will save the lame and gather the outcast, and I will turn their shame into praise and renown in all the earth.

7. At that time I will bring you in, Even at the time when I gather you together;
8. Indeed, <u>I will give you renown and praise among all the peoples of the earth, When I restore your fortunes before your eyes</u>, says the LORD" (Zeph. 3:14-20).

In His kingdom all will be restored to Israel as was eternally covenanted by God. They are His covenant people and He will carry out every detail of His covenanted promises. "Zephaniah 3:20. This verse summarizes Israel's yet-future blessings: regathering in the Promised Land (**home**), a favorable reputation (**honor and praise**; cf. v. 19) **among all the** nations, and a restoring of her **fortunes** (or a bringing back of her captives; cf. 2:7). This will all happen **before** her **very eyes.** In the Millennium, Israel will possess her land as God promised (Gen. 12:1–7; 13:14–17; 15:7–21; 17:7–8), and the Messiah, Israel's King, will establish His kingdom and will reign (2 Sam. 7:16; Ps. 89:3–4; Isa. 9:6–7; Dan. 7:27; Zeph. 3:15). To emphasize the divine authority of his message as well as the certainty of God's comfort, Zephaniah ended his book with the words, **says the LORD!**"[13]

Conclusion

It must be kept in focus that the day of the Lord is used as a technical term when referring to that time or day defined by Joel as well as the other prophets. The day of the Lord begins with His wrath on the entire creation. After His judgments then comes the restored covenanted Davidic kingdom with all the promised blessings with His people Israel. The greatest blessing is that Jesus will be in their midst. He is Israel's King, their Messiah. He will sovereignly reign from David's covenanted throne on the earth for 1,000 years.

---

[13]John D. Hannah, "Zephaniah" In , in *The Bible Knowledge Commentary: An Exposition of the Scriptures*, ed. J. F. Walvoord and R. B. Zuck (Wheaton, IL: Victor Books, 1985), Zep 3:20.

Zephaniah described a time of horrific and incomparable wrath. Then comes the time of great blessings, and this will only happen when His kingdom comes. The Scriptures are very accurate and very clear with all this.

"He will be great, and will be called the Son
of the Most High; and the Lord God will
give Him the throne of His father David; and
He will reign over the house of Jacob
forever; and His kingdom will have no end"
(Luke 1:32)

Chapter 5
The day of the Lord and other prophets and Peter

God's Word presents a vast amount of information concerning the day of the Lord. The major theme of Joel, Obadiah, and Zephaniah is the day of the Lord. Almost all the other prophets refer to this coming day in one way or another. Whether they speak of His coming wrath and unparalleled judgments or the times of His blessings in Christ's kingdom or the eternal state, the day of the Lord is major biblical doctrine.

There is no attempt here to present all the information given by the prophets on this coming day. Again, there is just a plethora of information on the day of the Lord in the Text. Some of these prophets do not use the term directly, but it is very obvious they are referring to it. Several examples will be presented.

Daniel

One such prophet is Daniel. Although he does not use this term, it is very obvious he is referring to that coming day.

- "Now at that time Michael, the great prince who stands *guard* over the sons of your people, will arise.
- And there will be a time of distress such as never occurred since there was a nation until that time;
- and at that time your people, everyone who is found written in the book, will be rescued.
- And many of those who sleep in the dust of the ground will awake, these to everlasting life, but the others to disgrace *and* everlasting contempt.
- And those who have insight will shine brightly like the brightness of the expanse of heaven, and those who lead the many to righteousness, like the stars forever and ever" (Dan. 12:1-3).

"And there will be a time of distress such as never occurred since there was a nation until that time." This is a direct reference to the unparalleled judgments in the day of the Lord. Joel refers to this (Joel 2:1-2) and so does Christ.[1] Note His very words which refer to this coming time. "For then there will be a great tribulation, such as has not occurred since the beginning of the world until now, nor ever shall. And unless those days had been cut short, no life would have been saved; but for the sake of the elect those days shall be cut short" (Mat. 24:21-22). Jesus makes it very clear that unless He returns there will no life left on the planet. He will return for the very purpose of delivering His covenanted people Israel in the day of the Lord. There also will be Gentiles those who helped Israel during this time of Christ's wrath (Mat. 25:31-46).

Daniel 12:1-3 presents at least two aspects of the day of the Lord and possibly three. The first is the unparalleled judgment that will come first and then the blessings of His kingdom. His kingdom or millennial reign when completed appears to merge into the eternal state. "And those who have insight will shine brightly like the brightness of the expanse of heaven, and those who lead the many to righteousness, like the stars forever and ever."

---

[1]This easily refers to Joel and the day of the Lord. "Blow a trumpet in Zion, and sound an alarm on My holy mountain! Let all the inhabitants of the land tremble, For the day of the LORD is coming; Surely it is near, a day of darkness and gloom, a day of clouds and thick darkness. As the dawn is spread over the mountains, so there is a great and mighty people; there has never been anything like it, nor will there be again after it to the years of many generations" (Joel 2:1-2). And even to Christ's own words: "But pray that your flight may not be in the winter, or on a Sabbath; for then there will be a great tribulation, such as has not occurred since the beginning of the world until now, nor ever shall" (Mat. 24:20-21). As has been noted previously, there will such great tribulation as has never occurred and this includes the flood of Gen. 6 – 9).

The day of the Lord includes:

- His coming wrath
- His coming kingdom
- The eternal state

"No doubt when the revelation contained in chapter 12 was given Daniel, he was concerned about his people's destiny. Now at the conclusion of this vision, the angel consoled Daniel by revealing two facts (vv. 1–3). First, the people of Israel (**your people**; cf. 9:24; 10:14) **will be delivered** by the intervention of **Michael** the angelic **prince** (cf. 10:13, 21), **who** is Israel's defender. In the Great Tribulation Satan will attempt to exterminate every descendant of Abraham… This **will be a time of** great unprecedented **distress** for Israel (cf. Matt. 24:21). Satan's attack against the people of the kingdom will be part of his effort to prevent the return and reign of Christ. The deliverance of Israel, Daniel's "people," refers not to individual salvation, though a remnant will be saved, but rather to national deliverance from subjugation to the Gentiles (cf. comments on "all Israel will be saved" in Rom. 11:26)… The second fact that consoled Daniel is the promise that those who sleep will be resurrected. Many Jews will lose their lives at the hands of Gentiles in the events revealed in chapter 11 (cf. Rev. 20:4)… Unbelieving Jews will be resurrected **to shame and everlasting contempt** and will not partake in the covenanted blessings. Jews, however, who believe the Messiah will be resurrected bodily **to everlasting life** and to positions of honor in Christ's millennial kingdom.[2]

---

[2]J. Dwight Pentecost, "Daniel" In , in *The Bible Knowledge Commentary: An Exposition of the Scriptures*, ed. J. F. Walvoord and R. B. Zuck (Wheaton, IL: Victor Books, 1985), Dan. 12:1–3.

Zechariah

Another example is Zechariah. He does not use the term the day of the Lord at all. Zechariah only uses the term 'that day.' It is very evident he is referring to that coming day i.e. the day of the Lord concerning both wrath and blessing. "The Lord's **coming** to **live among** Israel is messianic, referring to the time when the Messiah will come to rule on the throne of David. Possibly, however, both of Christ's advents are in view here as in passages such as Isaiah 9:6–7; 61:1–2. But the emphasis here is on the Second Advent when God's blessings on Israel will overflow to the nations. **That day** is a shortened way of referring to the future "day of the LORD" when He will come to judge the nations and fulfill His covenants with Israel in the millennial kingdom."[3]

The uses of 'that day' by Zechariah are listed below. There are more, but only the ones which can be *easily* designated in 'that day' as pertaining to His wrath or His kingdom are presented.

1) Zechariah 2:11 And many nations will join themselves to the LORD in that day and will become My people. Then I will dwell in your midst, and you will know that the LORD of hosts has sent Me to you. (*day of the Lord kingdom*)
2) Zechariah 3:10 In that day,' declares the LORD of hosts, 'every one of you will invite his neighbor to *sit* under *his* vine and under *his* fig tree. (*day of the Lord kingdom*)
3) Zechariah 9:16 And the LORD their God will save them in that day As the flock of His people; For *they are as* the stones of a crown, Sparkling in His land. (*day of the Lord kingdom*)
4) Zechariah 12:3 And it will come about in that day that I will make Jerusalem a heavy stone for all the peoples;

---

[3] F. Duane Lindsey, "Zechariah" In , in *The Bible Knowledge Commentary: An Exposition of the Scriptures*, ed. J. F. Walvoord and R. B. Zuck (Wheaton, IL: Victor Books, 1985), Zec 2:10–13.

all who lift it will be severely injured. And all the nations of the earth will be gathered against it. (*day of the Lord wrath*)

5) Zechariah 12:4 In that day," declares the LORD, "I will strike every horse with bewilderment, and his rider with madness. But I will watch over the house of Judah, while I strike every horse of the peoples with blindness. (*day of the Lord wrath*)

6) Zechariah 12:6 In that day I will make the clans of Judah like a firepot among pieces of wood and a flaming torch among sheaves, so they will consume on the right hand and on the left all the surrounding peoples, while the inhabitants of Jerusalem again dwell on their own sites in Jerusalem. (*day of the Lord wrath*)

7) Zechariah 12:8 In that day the LORD will defend the inhabitants of Jerusalem, and the one who is feeble among them in that day will be like David, and the house of David *will be* like God, like the angel of the LORD before them. (*day of the Lord wrath*)

8) Zechariah 12:9 And it will come about in that day that I will set about to destroy all the nations that come against Jerusalem. (*day of the Lord wrath*)

9) Zechariah 12:11 In that day there will be great mourning in Jerusalem, like the mourning of Hadadrimmon in the plain of Megiddo. (*day of the Lord wrath*)

10) Zechariah 14:4 And in that day His feet will stand on the Mount of Olives, which is in front of Jerusalem on the east; and the Mount of Olives will be split in its middle from east to west by a very large valley, so that half of the mountain will move toward the north and the other half toward the south.

11) Zechariah 14:6 And it will come about in that day that there will be no light; the luminaries will dwindle. (*day of the Lord wrath*)

12) Zechariah 14:8 And it will come about in that day that living waters will flow out of Jerusalem, half of them toward the eastern sea and the other half toward the

western sea; it will be in summer as well as in winter. (*day of the Lord kingdom*)

13) Zechariah 14:9 And the LORD will be king over all the earth; in <u>that day</u> the LORD will be *the only* one, and His name *the only* one. (*day of the Lord kingdom*)

14) Zechariah 14:13 And it will come about in <u>that day</u> that a great panic from the LORD will fall on them; and they will seize one another's hand, and the hand of one will be lifted against the hand of another. (*day of the Lord wrath*)

15) Zechariah 14:20 In <u>that day</u> there will *be inscribed* on the bells of the horses, "HOLY TO THE LORD." And the cooking pots in the LORD's house will be like the bowls before the altar. (*day of the Lord kingdom*)

16) Zechariah 14:21 And every cooking pot in Jerusalem and in Judah will be holy to the LORD of hosts; and all who sacrifice will come and take of them and boil in them. And there will no longer be a Canaanite in the house of the LORD of hosts in <u>that day</u>. (*day of the Lord kingdom*)

Peter

The epistle of second Peter presents another issue pertaining to the day of the Lord.

"But the day of the Lord will come like a thief, in which the heavens will pass away with a roar and the elements will be destroyed with intense heat, and the earth and its works will be burned up. Since all these things are to be destroyed in this way, what sort of people ought you to be in holy conduct and godliness, looking for and hastening the coming of the day of God, on account of which the heavens will be destroyed by burning, and the elements will melt with intense heat! But according to His promise we are looking for new heavens and a new earth, in which righteousness dwells. Therefore, beloved, since you look for these things, be diligent to be found by Him in peace, spotless and blameless" (2 Pet. 3:10-14).

It is sometimes hard to determine whether the day referred to in the Text is the millennial kingdom or that of the eternal state. It has been already noted there may be a merger of the two as the millennial kingdom will be transferred into the eternal state. "Then *comes* the end, when He delivers up the kingdom to the God and Father, when He has abolished all rule and all authority and power. For He must reign until He has put all His enemies under His feet" (1 Cor. 15:24-25).

"When the Lord does **come**, it will be both surprising and catastrophic: **like a thief.** This simile was used by Jesus (Matt. 24:42–44) and repeated by others (1 Thess. 5:2; Rev. 3:3; 16:15). **The day of the Lord** describes end-time events that begin after the Rapture and culminate with the commencement of eternity. In the middle of the 70th week of Daniel the Antichrist will turn against the people of God in full fury (Dan. 9:24–27…) In the catastrophic conflagration at the end of the Millennium, **the heavens** (the earth's atmosphere and the starry sky, not God's abode) **will disappear with a roar**, which in some way will involve fire (2 Peter 3:7, 12). **The elements** (*stoicheia*, either stars or material elements with which the universe is made) **will be destroyed by fire** (and will melt, v. 12), **and the earth and everything in it will be laid bare** (*eurethēsetai*)."[4]

---

[4]Kenneth O. Gangel, "2 Peter" In , in *The Bible Knowledge Commentary: An Exposition of the Scriptures*, ed. J. F. Walvoord and R. B. Zuck (Wheaton, IL: Victor Books, 1985), 2 Pet. 3:10.

Isaiah

Isaiah 65:17-25 presents a similar construction, that of possibly merging His millennial kingdom and reign into the eternal state.[5] It must be reminded that the millennial kingdom is prior to the eternal state of the new heavens and the new earth.

"Isaiah 65:17-25 is a description of the millennial kingdom, which is preliminary to the *new heavens and a new earth* (v. 17). Characteristics include Jerusalem being a joy instead of a burden (v. 18; cf. Zech. 12:2-3), longevity (Isa. 65:20; notice that sin will be punished in the Millennium), peace and security (vv. 21-23), and removing the animosity in nature (v. 25; cf. 11:7-9)."[6]

Conclusion

There are many references to the day of the Lord in all of the Scriptures. There are whole books which are dedicated

---

[5]"For behold, I create new heavens and a new earth; And the former things shall not be remembered or come to mind. But be glad and rejoice forever in what I create; For behold, I create Jerusalem *for* rejoicing, And her people *for* gladness. I will also rejoice in Jerusalem, and be glad in My people; And there will no longer be heard in her The voice of weeping and the sound of crying. No longer will there be in it an infant *who lives but a few* days, or an old man who does not live out his days; for the youth will die at the age of one hundred and the one who does not reach the age of one hundred shall be *thought* accursed. And they shall build houses and inhabit *them*; they shall also plant vineyards and eat their fruit. They shall not build, and another inhabit, they shall not plant, and another eat; for as the lifetime of a tree, *so shall be* the days of My people, And My chosen ones shall wear out the work of their hands. They shall not labor in vain, or bear *children* for calamity; for they are the offspring of those blessed by the LORD, And their descendants with them. It will also come to pass that before they call, I will answer; and while they are still speaking, I will hear. The wolf and the lamb shall graze together, and the lion shall eat straw like the ox; and dust shall be the serpent's food. They shall do no evil or harm in all My holy mountain," says the LORD" (Is. 65:17-25).

[6]Ryrie, Charles C., *The Ryrie Study Bible* (Chicago: Moody Press, 1978), 1110.

exclusively to the day of the Lord. His kingdom will come in the day of the Lord. The believer should be seeking a kingdom and an eternal state where His righteousness dwells.

1. "But the day of the Lord will come like a thief, in which the heavens will pass away with a roar and the elements will be destroyed with intense heat, and the earth and its works will be burned up.

2. Since all these things are to be destroyed in this way, what sort of people ought you to be in holy conduct and godliness,

3. looking for and hastening the coming of the day of God, on account of which the heavens will be destroyed by burning, and the elements will melt with intense heat!

4. *But according to His promise we are looking for new heavens and a new earth, in which righteousness dwell*" (2 Peter 3:10-14).

His Word always says it best!

Chapter 6
The day of the Lord and the church

The church

There are many issues which must be explored by the student of His Word concerning the day of the Lord. The warnings are many, and it is very clear that the church cannot go into this time of His wrath. The day of the Lord begins with the wrath of God which will come on an unbelieving world. Jesus will deliver His church from the coming wrath. The Thessalonians were told to "wait for His Son from heaven, whom He raised from the dead, *that is* Jesus, who delivers us from the wrath to come" (1 Thess. 1:10).

It is impossible for the church to go into the day of the Lord. Paul made this extremely clear that the church would be raptured *prior* to the day of the Lord.[1] The only book in the Word of God which identifies the actual beginning of the day of the Lord is in Second Thessalonians. Paul spelled this out very specifically in 2 Thess. 2:1-4 because the Thessalonians believed they might be in the day of the Lord. This was the main reason Second Thessalonians was written, because they thought they were in the day of the Lord.

1. "Now we request you, brethren, with regard to the coming of our Lord Jesus Christ, and our gathering

---

[1]"Now we request you, brethren, with regard to the coming of our Lord Jesus Christ, and our gathering together to Him, that you may not be quickly shaken from your composure or be disturbed either by a spirit or a message or a letter as if from us, to the effect that the day of the Lord has come. Let no one in any way deceive you, for *it will not come* unless **the apostasy comes first, and the man of lawlessness is revealed,** the son of destruction, who opposes and exalts himself above every so-called god or object of worship, so that he takes his seat in the temple of God, displaying himself as being God" (2 Thess. 2:1-4). These two events must take place before the day of the Lord begins. Once these two things occur, the day of the Lord has begun. The key to this is mostly the man of sin being revealed. Once he is revealed which will be after the rapture of the church, the day of the Lord has begun.

together to Him, (*The coming of the Lord Jesus is not the second coming in any sense; this coming is for the rapture of the church i.e. our gathering together to Him*)

2. That you may not be quickly shaken from your composure or be disturbed either by a spirit or a message or a letter as if from us, to the effect that the day of the Lord has come. (*The Thessalonians knew well the term and biblical doctrine of the day of the Lord. Apparently there were rumors, letters, or persons preaching that the day of the Lord had come. This was not possible and was nonsense. The day of the Lord cannot come until two things happen*)

3. Let no one in any way deceive you, for *it will not come* unless

    a. the apostasy comes first (*Most likely this has reference to the rapture of the church which must come first and Paul made this very clear*)[2]

    b. and the man of lawlessness is revealed, the son of destruction, who opposes and exalts himself above every so-called god or object of worship, so that he takes his seat in the temple of God, displaying himself as being God" (2 Thess. 2:1-4). (*The antichrist must be identified. Once these two things happen especially the latter i.e. the man of sin or antichrist identified, the day of the Lord has begun*)[3]

---

[2] It should be noted that there is one subordinating conjunction ἐὰν followed by two subjunctives. Unless these two things 'come' i.e. the apostasy and the man of sin revealed the day of the Lord had not begun in any sense. For more information please see this author's *The Greatness of Rapture,* "The Day of the Lord Begins Only After Two Very Specific Events," Tyndale Seminary Press.

[3] For much more detailed information on the rapture of the church please see this author's book titled *The Greatness of the Rapture* and subtitled *The Pre-Day of the Lord Rapture.*

The church cannot go into the day of Lord which begins with His coming wrath. He will deliver the church from His coming wrath by the rapture of His bride, the church. Then His wrath will begin after the man of sin or the antichrist is made known.

Conclusion

The day of the Lord is major biblical doctrine, and it would behoove any student of His Word to understand the great truths concerning this doctrine. Paul had taught the Thessalonians the doctrine of the day of the Lord well.

"Now as to the times and the epochs, brethren, you have no need of anything to be written to you. For you yourselves know full well that the day of the Lord will come just like a thief in the night. While they are saying, "Peace and safety!" then destruction will come upon them suddenly like birth pangs upon a woman with child; and they shall not escape. But you, brethren, are not in darkness, that the day should overtake you like a thief; for you are all sons of light and sons of day. We are not of night nor of darkness" (1 Thess. 5:1-5).

The church is not of the night and this should be understood very well. While they are saying, "Peace and safety!" then destruction will come upon them, never the church! He will deliver His bride from the wrath to come, prior to the day of the Lord. There should be no doubt with the rapture of the church occurring prior to the day of the Lord. The Scriptures are perfectly clear with this teaching and perfectly consistent.

For God has not destined us for wrath,
but for obtaining salvation through our
Lord Jesus Christ" (1 Thess. 5:9)

Chapter 7
Christ's Kingdom

God's biblical covenants define His Divine plan

A student of the Bible is often overwhelmed by the amount of information and data presented in theText. Since an infinite God has inerrantly revealed Himself to man by His Word, finite man has the responsibility to understand what God has revealed. God has revealed Himself and His purposes not in mystery enshrouded with secrecy, but in such a way that man is fully capable and culpable to understand what He has revealed. What is almost impossible to miss in Scripture in the midst of massive revelation are the biblical covenants which God has made with man. If Scripture is consistently understood as grammatically literal, that is using a normative use of the original languages, then there will be a sensible and consistent interpretation, especially concerning the biblical covenants.

The biblical covenants are the true basis and foundation for God's entire sovereign and theocratic plan[1] with mankind. They are often overlooked in theology and this causes much confusion concerning His covenanted kingdom program. These covenants are the vehicle in which God rests His complete redemptive, prophetic, and kingdom program.[2]   Unless there is

---

[1] *Plan* by definition is a scheme of action, or design, or arrangement; such as *'he has an elaborate plan.'* A *program* by definition may be a plan but usually includes a schedule to be followed. One entering a church service is usually given a *program* that may be part of how the service was *planned.* The terms may be interchangeable but there is a difference.

[2] God has revealed His *entire* redemptive kingdom program for Israel that is *biblically covenanted* with Israel but includes all men, *the Gentiles, the nations of the world.*. Paul addresses and expounds on this exact issue that is foundationally based on the Abrahamic covenant; the promise of salvation to the Gentiles or the nations, that faith alone saves, the offer of grace to the nations is full lodged in the Abrahamic covenant. See Galatians 3:6-18 especially vs. 8. All biblical prophecy stems from the biblical covenants. His *kingdom program* spoken of in Scripture is always fully derived from His biblically covenanted plan and program with Israel.

a thorough knowledge and acceptance of God's biblical covenants, then confusion results in the outworking of His total program revealed in Scripture.

The biblical covenants that are of most concern are the Abrahamic, the land, the Davidic, the new, and the Mosaic. All but the Mosaic are eternal, unconditional, and unilateral, that is dependent on God alone to carry out all the promises that are in these covenants. In reference to the covenanted kingdom, the concern lies in the Abrahamic, land, David, and the new covenants. These biblical covenants define the Davidic throne and kingdom.

These biblical covenants are the fountainhead from which God's entire redemptive kingdom program springs forth. The biblical covenants as clearly written reveals the covenanted people, the covenanted nation, the covenanted land, the covenanted seed, the covenanted house, the covenanted throne, the covenanted kingdom, the covenanted king, the covenanted reign, the covenanted redemption, the covenanted cleansing, the covenanted Spirit, the list goes on and on into much more depth and detail.   In the bible, any reference to Israel is always the covenanted Jewish nation Israel by God's design and definition. This is not because God simply declared it, but by God's biblical covenant promises and oaths, they, the Jews, are solely His covenanted people and none other.[3] This is why Israel was know and identified as His covenant people never the church.

---

[3]By God's own oath bound covenants with Israel, it is utterly impossible for God to abandon the nation Israel, the Jews. There are many similar passages that can be referenced here. It seems it would be well advised for any form of replacement theology to be more prudent about what it advocates about the nation Israel. "For you are a holy people to the Lord your God; the Lord your God has chosen you to be a people for His own possession out of all the peoples who are on the face of the earth. The Lord did not set His love on you nor choose you because you were more in number than any of the peoples, for you were the fewest of all peoples, but because the Lord loved you and kept the oath which He swore to your forefathers, the Lord brought you out by a mighty hand and redeemed you from the house of slavery, from the hand of Pharaoh king of Egypt" (Dt. 7:6-8); "I am the Lord, your Holy One, The Creator of Israel, your King" (Isa. 43:15); "I, even I, am the one

Gentiles i.e. the nations were never God's biblically covenanted people in any sense (Eph. 2:11-12). This does not mean that there are not great promises made to the Gentiles. There are very great promises to the Gentiles in Scripture. Justification by faith alone[4] was promised in the Abrahamic covenant to the nations (Gal. 3:8), but the Abrahamic covenant itself is not made with the Gentiles. Even though this promise was made in the Abrahamic covenant, it is carried out by Christ Himself in the new covenant by His blood of the new covenant. Even kings were promised in the Abrahamic covenant (Gen. 17:6), yet the kingdom was covenanted with David (2 Sam. 7:12-16). One has to respect all the details of these eternal covenants.

The Father has sworn to carry out His sovereign plan, purposes, program, and design in and through the nation Israel, the Jew, that is national Israel. The nation Israel, the Jews, are His chosen people and nation, designated and protected by the biblical covenants[5] elected by Him as the recipients of the

---

who wipes out your transgressions for My own sake, And I will not remember your sins" (Isa. 43:25); "I will dwell among the sons of Israel, and will not forsake My people Israel" (1 Kings 6:13); "For I, the Lord, do not change; therefore you, O sons of Jacob, are not consumed" (Mal. 3:6).
[4]"Even so Abraham believed God, and it was reckoned to him as righteousness. Therefore, be sure that it is those who are of faith who are sons of Abraham. The Scripture, foreseeing that God would justify the Gentiles by faith, preached the gospel beforehand to Abraham, saying, all the nations will be blessed in you. So then those who are of faith are blessed with Abraham, the believer" (Gal. 3:6-9).
[5] No Gentile nation or people have this kind of promised covenanted protection. Even the Church has not one promise covenanted such as this unless one holds to some form of replacement for the nation Israel. This promise is reserved exclusively for the house of Israel because God's biblically covenanted program will be fulfilled in them and through the nation Israel exclusively. As part of the Abrahamic covenant: "And I will bless those who bless you, and the one who curses you I will curse. And in you all the families of the earth will be blessed" (Gen. 12:3). As attached to the new covenant: "Thus says the Lord, Who gives the sun for light by day And the fixed order of the moon and the stars for light by night, Who stirs up the sea so that its waves roar; The Lord of hosts is His name: If this fixed order departs From before Me, declares the Lord, Then the offspring of

biblical covenants which are ultimately sealed with His Son's blood (Heb. 9:11-28). To ignore or replace any aspect of the biblical covenants to include replacing His covenanted people Israel with the church or any other people is to create havoc in interpretation and do absolute and total violence to the Word of God.

What is frequently missing in a study of theology is not only a consistent literal interpretation of Scripture, especially that of the covenants with Israel, but also the very specific details of the biblical covenants. If taken literally, not one iota or tittle of God's biblically covenanted promises may be understood as less than fully and completely antitypical. The many promises embodied in the oath-bound covenants never speak of types or allegory because no one would be able to comprehend such veiled typological language. The covenants speak to real men to whom real promises were made including a literal salvation, a literal land with a literal Jewish throne and kingdom. If this were not so one might spiritualize the land, the kingdom and possible place David's throne in heaven which is totally unbiblical. There is absolutely no biblical support for such in all the Text.

All of this is not difficult when one is certain of the inerrancy and literalness of the Scriptures. One must be consistent with a literal interpretation that is simply the normal use of the language/s as posited in the Text. Either God's covenants must be literally fulfilled, or the interpretation is quite literally in the hands of the interpreter. This appears to be the case today with much exegesis. Let Scripture be its own interpreter, as it is designed to be. It is a complete denial of biblical truth to say that any or all of the eternal biblical covenants have been fulfilled to all the recipients mentioned in the covenants in and through the nation Israel. The Scriptures are very clear in this matter and extremely consistent in the use

---

Israel also will cease From being a nation before Me forever. Thus says the Lord, If the heavens above can be measured And the foundations of the earth searched out below, Then I will also cast off all the offspring of Israel For all that they have done," declares the Lord" (Jer. 31:35-37).

and interpretation of the biblical covenants and prophecies directly related to them.

The church is often assumed to be the capstone, the epitome, the archetype,[6] fulfilling God's redemptive kingdom

---

[6] "The covenant with Abraham. With Abraham we enter upon a new epoch in the Old Testament revelation of the covenant of grace. There are several points that deserve attention here: up to the time of Abraham there was no formal establishment of the covenant of grace. While Gen. 3:15 already contains the elements of this covenant, it does not record a formal transaction by which the covenant was established. It does not even speak explicitly of a covenant. The establishment of the covenant with Abraham marked the beginning of an institutional Church. In pre-Abrahamic times there was what may be called "the church in the house." There were families in which the true religion found expression, and undoubtedly also gatherings of believers, but there was no definitely marked body of believers, separated from the world, that might be called the Church.' Louis Berkhof, *Systematic Theology* (Grand Rapids: Eerdmans Publishing, 1979), 295. 'In the New Testament.' The New Testament Church is essentially one with the Church of the old dispensation. As far as their essential nature is concerned, they both consist of true believers, and of true believers only. And in their external organization both represent a mixture of good and evil. Yet several important changes resulted from the accomplished work of Jesus Christ. The Church was divorced from the national life of Israel and obtained an independent organization. In connection with this the national boundaries of the Church were swept away. What had up to this time been a national Church now assumed a universal character." Louis Berkhof, *Systematic Theology*, 571.

plan[7] and program[8] as espoused by most forms of covenant theology, replacement theology,[9] or its various counterparts.

---

[7] "The Roman Church took up the idea of Augustine and identified the church with the kingdom of God, but it also went a step farther in identifying the kingdom of God with its own ecclesiastical organization. As Berkhof states: "Augustine viewed the kingdom as a present reality and identified it with the pious and holy, that is, with the church as a community of believers; but he used some expressions which seem to indicate that he also saw it embodied in the episcopally organized Church. The Roman Catholic Church frankly identified the Kingdom of God with their hierarchical institution. Under amillennial influence, then, the kingdom of God was divorced from its connection with the millennial reign of Christ following the Second Advent, separated from the nation Israel, and made identical to the church in the present age, and specifically identified with the Roman Church. The process by which this was accomplished involved the spiritualization of the Old Testament's promises to Israel, denying some, translating others into the Roman Church. The stark contrast of what the Roman Church is as compared to the millennial kingdom illustrates the extremes to which spiritualization of Scripture can go. In the Reformation the Reformers seem to have returned somewhat to the position of Augustine. This is defined by Berkhof as a denial to the Roman position that the kingdom of God is identical to the visible church, i.e., the whole company of believers. This is essentially the position of amillennial conservatives today." John F Walvoord, *The Millennial Kingdom* (Grand Rapids: Zondervan, 1959), 99.

[8]This can hardly be assumed biblically true even in the first century as Christ Himself has some very great and negative things to say about the first century churches especially five of those in Revelation chapter two and three. "To the angel of the **church in Ephesus** write: The One who holds the seven stars in His right hand, the One who walks among the seven golden lampstands, says this:…'But I have this against you, that **you have left your first love**" (Rev. 2:1; 4); "And to the angel of the **church in Pergamum** write: The One who has the sharp two-edged sword says this: … **But I have a few things against you**, because you have there some who **(note: all the false teachings)** hold the **teaching** of Balaam, who kept **teaching** Balak to put a stumbling block before the sons of Israel, to eat things sacrificed to idols, and to commit acts of immorality. 'Thus you also have some who in the same way hold the **teaching** of the Nicolaitans" (Rev. 2:12; 14-15); "And to the angel of the **church in Thyatira** write: The Son of God, who has eyes like a flame of fire, and His feet are like burnished bronze, says this: '**But I have this against you,** that **you tolerate the woman Jezebel**, who calls herself a prophetess, and she teaches and leads My bond-servants astray, so that they commit acts of immorality and eat things sacrificed to idols" (Rev. 2:18; 20); "And to the angel of the **church**

The church is often assumed to be in the kingdom of God or is the kingdom of God in some form understanding only the rule of Christ not the biblically covenanted Jewish throne and kingdom of Israel from which Christ must rule. This leads to many church-kingdom theories and theologies. The biblical distinctions between the church and Israel become continually blurred and obscured by theorists trying to accommodate their own or another theology. Berkhof makes this statement:

> The Church and the Kingdom of God… The idea of the kingdom of God. The Kingdom of God is primarily an eschatological concept. The fundamental idea of the Kingdom in Scripture is not that of a restored theocratic kingdom of God in Christ – which is essentially a kingdom of Israel--, as the Premillenarians claim; neither is it a new social condition, pervaded by the Spirit of Christ, and realized by man through such as external means as good laws, civilization, education, social reforms, and so on, as the Modernists would have us believe. The primary idea of the Kingdom of God in Scripture is that of the rule of God established and acknowledged in the hearts of sinners by the powerful regenerating influence of the Holy Spirit, insuring them of the inestimable blessings of salvation, -- a rule that is realized in principle on earth, but will not reach its culmination until the

---

in Sardis write: He who has the seven Spirits of God, and the seven stars, says this: 'I know your deeds, that you have a name that you are alive, but you are dead" (Rev. 3:1). "And to the angel of the church in Laodicea write: The Amen, the faithful and true Witness, the Beginning of the creation of God, says this: 'I know your deeds, that you are neither cold nor hot; I would that you were cold or hot. 'So because you are lukewarm, and neither hot nor cold, I will spit you out of My mouth" (Rev. 3:14-16).

[9] Any theology that replaces the nation Israel, the Jews with the church primarily or any other people or any other theological system is replacement theology. Israel is defined and guarded by the biblical covenants.

visible and glorious return of Jesus Christ. The
present realization of it is spiritual and invisible.
Jesus took hold of this eschatological concept
and made it prominent in his teachings. He
clearly taught the present spiritual realization and
the universal character of the Kingdom.
Moreover, He Himself effected that realization in
a measure formerly unknown and greatly
increased the present blessings of the Kingdom.
At the same time He held out the blessed hope of
the future appearance of that Kingdom in
external glory and with the perfect blessings of
salvation.[10]

Certain theologies seem to believe some form of a
church-kingdom theory not understanding or consistently
interpreting the great biblical distinctives between the true
nature of Israel and the true nature of the church. Israel is a
biblically covenanted and defined nation and people. This
distinction is not only biblical but absolutely essential to basic
hermeneutics. To ignore these distinctions may be very
convenient to one's theological system, but falls short of good
exegesis and being scripturally accurate. There is great
distinction between the biblically defined church and the
covenanted Jewish theocratic throne and kingdom with Israel.
A very specific theocratic ordering is demanded by the biblical
covenants. George Peters addresses this exact problem many
times in his monumental work, *The Theocratic Kingdom*.

The Church is not like the Kingdom of God once
established, *lacking*[11] the Theocratic arrangement
once instituted.... The Church is not like the
Kingdom once established *overthrown and*

---

[10] Louis Berkhof, *Systematic Theology*, 568.
[11] Italics or capital letters (or variations in spelling) in *all quotes or direct
quotes* are by each author.

promised a restoration.... The Church is not the
Kingdom, otherwise the disciples were *ignorant*
of what they preached... that the Church is the
promised Kingdom is opposed *by the covenants*
... the preaching of the Kingdom as nigh and
then its *postponement* is against making the
Church a Kingdom... The simple fact is, that if
we once take the covenanted promises in their
plain sense, and view the testimony of Scripture
sustaining such a sense, it is *utterly impossible* to
convert the Church into the promised Kingdom
without a *violation* of propriety and unity of
Divine Purpose.[12]

Division/s over the covenants

In the history of the church, there has been division over
biblical covenants knowingly or unknowingly. The question is
not whether there are covenants, but what *are* the actual
covenants, and which ones may apply, and perhaps which ones
do not. This frequently relates to replacement theology and/or
preterism[13] or various forms of preterism.

Covenant theology replaces or overrides the biblical
covenants by two or three undefined covenants it believes are
biblical.[14] Covenant theologians believe their covenants are

---

[12] George N. H. Peters, *The Theocratic Kingdom*, 3 vols. (Grand Rapids:
Kregel Publications, 1988), 1:612.

[13] The basis definition of *preterism* according to Webster's Encyclopedic
Dictionary is 'maintaining that the prophecies in the Apocalypse have
already been fulfilled.' While the term seems to be evolving as relating also
to partial preterism, most who are preterists see or understand God's
program for Israel as somehow fulfilled or to some degree partially or totally
fulfilled. What is tragic is that many of preterists are looking only to
prophecy that is admitted essential, but they are not confining themselves in
anyway to biblical covenants from which prophecy emerges especially
concerning the Jew or national Israel.

[14] According to Berkhof 'wherever we have the essential elements of a
covenant, namely contracting parties, a promise or promises, and a
condition, there we have a covenant' (p266, B. 3.). He goes on to define the

biblical and extant, and the basis for God's program. It is claimed that covenant theology sees or understands that the ultimate goal of man in history is for the glory of God, and without further scrutiny, this claim would be quite acceptable. However, covenant theology analyzed reveals the glory of God *might* be the intended goal, but this goal and glory rests/abides in the church that is in the redemption of the elect.[15] There were and will be different groups of the elect not just one. A scriptural example is God's remnant in the nation Israel. Biblically, the remnant will always be Jews from the nation of Israel, unless some theology redefines the nation Israel or the Jew. Therefore, in covenant theology there is effectively one gospel and one covenant. "The Bible teaches that there is but a single gospel by which men can be saved. And because the gospel is nothing but the revelation of the covenant of grace, it follows that there is also but one covenant. This gospel was already in the maternal promise, Gen. 3:15, was preached unto Abraham, Gal. 3:8, and may not be supplanted by any Judaistic gospel, Gal. 1:8,9."[16]

In covenant theology, the covenant of grace dominates their entire theological system, and nothing but nothing is

---

Covenant of Redemption, the basis for the Covenant of Grace (p270, E. 2.) But he admits that 'it is not easy to determine precisely who the second part is' in the Covenant of Grace (p 273). To base an entire theological system on covenants defined with no complete and specific clarity would seem to encourage those who hold to such a system to rethink their position on what are *the true Biblical covenants*. Quotes from Louis Berkhof, *Systematic Theology* (Grand Rapid: Eerdmans Publishing, 1979).

[15] "From the point of view of election... According to some theologians the Church is the *community of the elect*, the *coetus electorum*. This definition is apt to be somewhat misleading, however. It applies only to the Church *ideally* considered, the Church as it exists in the idea of God and as it will be completed at the end of the ages, and not to the Church as a present empirical reality. Election includes all those who belong to the body of Christ, irrespective of their present actual relation to it. But the elect who are yet unborn, or who are still strangers in Christ and outside the pale of the Church, cannot be said to belong to the Church *realiter*." Berkhof, *Systematic Theology*, 567.

[16] Ibid., 279.

allowed to violate it. Dr. John Walvoord has this to say about the covenant of grace:

> All events of the created world are designed to manifest the glory of God. The error of covenant theologians is that they combine all the many facets of divine purpose in the one objective of fulfillment of the covenant of grace. From a logical standpoint, this is the reductive error --- the use of one aspect of the whole as the determining element. The dispenational view of Scripture taken as a whole is far more satisfactory as it allows for the literal and natural interpretation of the great covenants of Scripture, in particular those with Abraham, Moses, David, and with Israel as a whole and explains them in the light of their own historical and prophetical context without attempting to conform them to a theological concept to which they are mostly unsuited. This explanation fully sustains the fundamental thesis of Calvinism, that God is sovereign and all will in the end manifest His glory. The various purposes of God for Israel, for the church which is His body, for the Gentile nations, for the unsaved, for Satan and the wicked angels, for the earth and for the heavens have each their contribution. How impossible it is to compress all of these factors into the mold of the covenant of grace.[17]

"The covenant of grace may be defined as that gracious agreement between the offended God and the offending but elect sinner, in which God promises salvation through faith in Christ, and the sinner accepts this believingly, promising a life

---

[17] John F. Walvoord, *The Millennial Kingdom* (Grand Rapids: Zondervan Publishing, 1959), 92.

of faith and obedience."[18] "The idea of a transcendent purpose and provision, which is spoken of in Christian literature as the "Covenant of Grace" or of "Redemption," underlies the whole of Written Revelation."[19]

While covenant theology may deny salvation or redemption of the elect as the ultimate goal, this is covenant theology's salvific end and purpose, totally based on a covenant or covenants which are believed to be biblical. But to place full confidence in covenants which are not literally spelled out in Scripture, and not to place full confidence in the biblical covenants which are eternal, unconditional, unilateral, and literally and inerrantly spelled out over and over again in Scripture, is to violate most rules of interpretation. "Covenant theology is definitely a product of theological theory rather than biblical exposition. While covenant theologians such as Berkhof labor over many Scriptural proofs, the specific formulas of the covenants are inductions from Calvinistic theology which go beyond the Scriptures. Charles Hodge, a covenant theologian, states plainly: "God entered into covenant with Adam. This statement does not rest upon any express declaration of the Scriptures."[20] Not only is there great misunderstanding of the biblical covenants, but also concerning their nature and the use or the outworking of the biblical covenants. George Peters comments:

> The reader will carefully regard this matter, as it is essential to a correct understanding of much Scripture. It is a sad fact, that more ignorance and misunderstanding exist in relation to the covenants than perhaps of any other portion of the Bible. This originates from the manner in which the subject has been handled by theologians of talent and eminence. Instead of

---

[18] Berkhof, *Systematic Theology*, 277.
[19] Roderick Campbell, *Israel and the New Covenant* (Philadelphia: Presbyterian and Reformed Publishing Company, 1954), 25.
[20] John F. Walvoord, *The Millennial Kingdom*, 88.

confining themselves to the covenants in which man is directly interested and which have been directly given to him by God, they have much to say concerning "a covenant of Redemption" entered into by the Father and Son from eternity (and undertake to give the particulars of what is not on record), and "a Covenant of Grace" (which embraces the particulars of salvation, etc.) but the distinctive Abrahamic Covenant and the manner in which it is confirmed is left without due consideration. This introduces a series of wild and fanciful interpretations, such as that all nations are now in the position once occupied by the Jewish nation; that God does not regard the Jewish nation with more favor that other nations; that the promises to the Jewish nation are typical, temporary, conditional, etc. Believing that we are under an entire New Covenant (which they cannot point out in the Scriptures, but which they affirm is this or that, viz.: this dispensation or the sacrifice of Christ, or the tender of Salvation to all believers, etc.), they, of course, ignore the *necessity* of our becoming "the seed of Abraham, of our being engrafted, etc. The relationship that believers sustain to the Jewish nation is utterly misapprehended, and inevitable confusion and antagonism arise…. It is painful to notice the discrepancies, amid a show of profound learning and speculation.[21]

All the biblical covenants if taken literally describe and clearly define but one covenanted people and nation and that is the Jewish nation Israel. All the biblical covenants if taken literally describe but one covenanted Jewish throne and

---

[21]Peters, *The Theocratic Kingdom*, 1:320.

kingdom. All the biblical covenants if taken literally describe a single unity of purpose and design to events in world history as understood in the Scriptures revealed in the progressive revelation of the Scriptures.[22] All the biblical books of the prophets and their prophecies, which ultimately flow from God's biblically covenanted program, describe but one covenanted Jewish throne and kingdom.

Against the accusation of being just too pedantic or too Jewish about the details of the biblical covenants, it must be

---

[22]A student of the Word expects progressive events in world history toward an expected and definitive end, as is given by the progressive revelation of the Scriptures. This is completely revealed as an unfolding of eschatological truth with its basis in the biblical covenants. The reason this is true by events revealed as designed in progressive revelation is that the ages were specifically prepared by God and spelled out for our understanding. Christ is not only the immanent Agent of creation of the tangible earth and all its related systems as is visibly seen but also the ages and times, all the events in world History. "For by Him all things were created, both in the heavens and on earth, **visible and invisible, whether thrones or dominions or rulers or authorities—all things have been created by Him and for Him.**" ὅτι ἐν αὐτῷ ἐκτίσθη τὰ πάντα ἐν τοῖς οὐρανοῖς καὶ ἐπὶ τῆς γῆς, **τὰ ὁρατὰ καὶ τὰ ἀόρατα**, εἴτε θρόνοι εἴτε κυριότητες εἴτε **ἀρχαὶ εἴτε ἐξουσίαι· τὰ πάντα δι' αὐτοῦ καὶ εἰς αὐτὸν ἔκτισται**" (Col. 1:16); "By faith we understand that **the worlds** were prepared by the word of God, so that what is seen was not made out of things which are visible" (Hebrews 11:3). Πίστει νοοῦμεν κατηρτίσθαι **τοὺς αἰῶνας** ῥήματι θεοῦ, εἰς τὸ μὴ ἐκ φαινομένων τὸ βλεπόμενον γεγονέναι." The ages or worlds are **τοὺς αἰῶνας** (αἰών, ῶνος,—a period of existence: **1.** one's lifetime, life,. **2.** an age, generation, posterity,. **3.** a long space of time, an age, **4.** a definite space of time, an era, epoch, age.. Liddell, H, A lexicon : Abridged from Liddell and Scott's Greek-English lexicon , (Oak Harbor, WA: Logos Research Systems, Inc., 1996), 25. For He is the God of all history. "Thus says the Lord, the King of Israel And his Redeemer, the Lord of hosts: **'I am the first and I am the last,** and there is no God besides Me. 'And who is like Me? Let him proclaim and declare it; yes, let him recount it to Me in order, From the time that I established the ancient nation. And let them declare to them the things that are coming And the events that are going to take place" (Isaiah 44:6-7). Thus He is truly the Alpha and Omega who designed the ages, "**I am the Alpha and the Omega,**" says the Lord God, "who is and who was and who is to come, the Almighty " Ἐγώ εἰμι τὸ ἄλφα καὶ τὸ ὦ, λέγει κύριος ὁ θεός, ὁ ὢν καὶ ὁ ἦν καὶ ὁ ἐρχόμενος, ὁ παντοκράτωρ" (Rev. 1:8).

remembered that Jesus as the Jewish Messiah (Christ) has His covenanted position described in detail by the biblical covenants.[23] This is what the Jewish throne and kingdom are all about, Jesus is the Jewish Messiah (the Christ), the Anointed One who must reign from David's throne over the Jewish kingdom.[24] The biblical covenants must be literally and completely fulfilled, for Christ must reign in this identical theocratic kingdom for the covenants to be fulfilled. This is why there is Christ's command to seek this kingdom first.[25] This is His coming kingdom which His disciples were taught to pray for. This will put all things into great focus concerning God's program from Adam. Christ is the last Adam and He will reign in His covenanted kingdom as the covenanted King with all the redeemed from Adam by His covenanted blood. This is not the church in any sense although the church will reign with Him.

There is a massive amount of details related to the Person of the Jewish Messiah concerning His covenanted position especially His essential genealogy[26] as the covenanted

---

[23] It must be kept in mind that all biblical prophecy about the Messiah will never contradict the biblical covenants, but will arise and flow from them.

[24] "Whoever believes that **Jesus is the Christ** is born of God, and whoever loves the Father loves the child born of Him" (1 John 5:1); Πᾶς ὁ πιστεύων ὅτι Ἰησοῦς ἐστιν ὁ Χριστὸς, ἐκ τοῦ θεοῦ γεγέννηται, καὶ πᾶς ὁ ἀγαπῶν τὸν γεννήσαντα ἀγαπᾷ [καὶ] τὸν γεγεννημένον ἐξ αὐτοῦ." 'One must believe Jesus is the Christ' is really the basis for the Gospel. Jesus is the anointed to sit on David's literal covenanted throne not some throne in heaven.. Note the articulation in the statement Ἰησοῦς ἐστιν ὁ Χριστὸς.

[25] "But seek first His kingdom and His righteousness, and all these things will be added to you" (Mat. 6:33); ζητεῖτε δὲ πρῶτον τὴν βασιλείαν [τοῦ θεοῦ] καὶ τὴν δικαιοσύνην αὐτοῦ, καὶ ταῦτα πάντα προστεθήσεται ὑμῖν. Note the present active imperative... ζητεῖτε δὲ πρῶτον τὴν βασιλείαν [τοῦ θεοῦ] καὶ τὴν δικαιοσύνην αὐτοῦ, this is very significant as to the foremost priority Jesus puts on the kingdom. You want a life, καὶ ταῦτα πάντα will be added, so seek the kingdom! For He is the anointed of the biblically covenanted kingdom. All are to seek or strive for this kingdom.

[26] Why have the NT begin with such a technical genealogy if the literally covenanted Jewish throne of Israel were not being promised to the literal genealogical proven son of David (completely referring to the Davidic

Heir to the covenanted Davidic throne and kingdom. This is why Messiah's genealogy is so critical (Mat. 1:1-17), as He is by biblically covenanted decree the Davidic Jewish Heir Apparent to the Jewish throne and kingdom.

Based on the biblical covenants, especially the Davidic, the Davidic throne and kingdom by covenanted[27] and

---

throne and kingdom as defined by the Davidic covenant). Jesus as the literal son of David inherits David's throne through Joseph. Note: the emphasis on the Son of David as coming first in Matthew's genealogy and then the son of Abraham through David. Jesus is not only David's son as Heir to David's literal throne and kingdom but also inherits the world or nations through the literal Abrahamic covenant as being its Heir Apparent. "The record of the genealogy of Jesus the Messiah, **the son of David, the son of Abraham**: Abraham was the father of Isaac, Isaac the father of Jacob, and Jacob the father of Judah and his brothers. Judah was the father of Perez and Zerah by Tamar, Perez was the father of Hezron, and Hezron the father of Ram. Ram was the father of Amminadab, Amminadab the father of Nahshon, and Nahshon the father of Salmon. Salmon was the father of Boaz by Rahab, Boaz was the father of Obed by Ruth, and Obed the father of Jesse. <u>Jesse was **the father of David the king**</u>. David was the father of **Solomon** by Bathsheba who had been the wife of Uriah. Solomon was the father of **Rehoboam**, Rehoboam the father of **Abijah**, and Abijah the father of **Asa**. Asa was the father of **Jehoshaphat**, Jehoshaphat the father of **Joram**, and Joram the father of **Uzziah**. Uzziah was the father of Jotham, Jotham the father of Ahaz, and Ahaz the father of **Hezekiah**. Hezekiah was the father of **Manasseh**, Manasseh the father of **Amon**, and Amon the father of **Josiah**. Josiah became the father of **Jeconiah** and his brothers, at the time of the deportation to Babylon. After the deportation to Babylon: Jeconiah became the father of Shealtiel, and Shealtiel the father of Zerubbabel. Zerubbabel was the father of Abihud, Abihud the father of Eliakim, and Eliakim the father of Azor. Azor was the father of Zadok, Zadok the father of Achim, and Achim the father of Eliud. Eliud was the father of Eleazar, Eleazar the father of Matthan, and Matthan the father of Jacob. Jacob was the father of Joseph the husband of Mary, by whom Jesus was born, who is called the Messiah" (Mat. 1-16).

[27]"When your days are complete and you lie down with your fathers, I will raise up your **descendant** after you, who will come forth from you, and I will establish **his kingdom**. "He shall build a house for My name, and I will establish the throne of his kingdom forever. "I will be a father to him and he will be a son to Me; when he commits iniquity, I will correct him with the rod of men and the strokes of the sons of men, but My lovingkindness shall not depart from him, as I took it away from Saul, whom I removed from

antitypical design, cannot be changed even minutely without vitiating the original intent of His archetypal plan, purpose, and goal.[28] If this were possible, which is it not,[29] then perhaps God is not able to carry out His program designed around the Jewish nation Israel, or He has deceived Israel and the nations and never intended to do so. Or has He completely abandoned His oath-bound covenants sealed with blood sacrifice, and even swore by His own Person and holiness[30] to carry out?

Assuming this premise, then the original biblical covenants based on God's promises and oaths were never given as antitypical and never to be understood as literal to be carried out exactly in every detail as He promised. If any of this were true which it most definitely is not, that is God departing or abandoning in any sense His original biblical covenants, as certain writers and theologians confidently assert, this would violate, vitiate, and abrogate effectively everything God has

---

before you. **"Your house and your kingdom shall endure before Me forever; your throne shall be established forever"** (2 Samuel 7:12-16). The emphasis is on your house and kingdom and your throne. 7:16 :עַד־עוֹלָם וְנֶאְמַן בֵּיתְךָ וּמַמְלַכְתְּךָ עַד־עוֹלָם לְפָנֶיךָ כִּסְאֲךָ יִהְיֶה נָכוֹן עַד־עוֹלָם note the עַד־עוֹלָם Which is literally *until forever or until eternity*.

[28] Some do this by placing David's throne in heaven. This is not possible in any sense if one is to remain true to a consistently literal exegesis and interpretation of the Text especially the God ordained Davidic covenant. With reference to the 'already not yet' allusion or better illusion, there is no already 'Davidic throne' during the church age. However, the identical Davidic throne will be restored over Israel in Jerusalem in His kingdom, *never* in heaven. There is absolutely no basis and no Text for such interpretation in God's Word except by a whim.

[29] Romans 11:28-29. "From the standpoint of the gospel they are enemies for your sake, but from the standpoint of God's choice they are beloved for the sake of the fathers; for the gifts and the calling of God are **irrevocable**" (Rom. 11:25-29). While there is a blindness and hardness at this time with the nation Israel, it would be dangerous theology to say God has replaced or abandoned them. This passage makes it very obvious He has not! The Lord has made it very clear He will never ever abandon Israel, the house of Jacob, the Jews. "For I, the Lord, do not change; therefore **you, O sons of Jacob, are not consumed**" (Malachi 3:6).

[30] "Once I have sworn by My holiness; I will not lie to David" (Psalm 89:35).

declared in His Word. This impugns the very character, nature, and faithfulness of God. How utterly inconceivable are the arrogance and audacity of those who do not just simply accept the promises God has declared and proven to be true by His Word. It would seem many more teachers and students of the Word would be more reticent about making bold assertions about which they are so confident, if they relied more on the inerrant words of Scripture and details rather than on any errant theological system.

To replace Israel in any way with any other people, nation, or theology is to violate the truths and promises of all the biblical covenants and prophecies in the Word of God. The church is not defined or described by any of the biblical covenants or prophecies save one. That given by Christ Himself: "And I also say to you that you are Peter, and upon this rock I will build My church; and the gates of Hades shall not overpower it" (Mat 16:18). Only Christ can build His church, His body, and that is what He is doing today. Israel was never designated as His body. He build His church, Israel is by covenant design.

The biblical covenants are made with an identifiable people

Pertaining to the Jewish people, even a basic understanding of Judaism, is the realization that the biblical covenants are primarily with Israel. While this fundamental understanding may vary within Judaism itself, it is a basic tenet for its outworking for biblical Judaism.

> God made covenants with a particular people that they should be His priesthood. To this people, the seed of Abraham, the slaves He had just redeemed from Egypt, He revealed the Torah, the Law which they were to obey, as the particular burden of the Jews and the sign of their unique destiny in the world. He chose the land of Canaan as His inheritance and that of His people, the Holy Land which would forever

remain the place in which He would most clearly be manifest..... God's initial covenant with Abraham, was with the head of a family, and the Jewish people was conceived as the every-increasing number of his descendants. Hence to this day the convert to Judaism is not only accepted into the faith; the ritual prescribes that he be adopted into the family as a child of Abraham.... The covenant with God binds the Jewish people to the task of being a corporate priesthood. God redeemed them from slavery in Egypt, let them hear His voice, led them to the promised land and vowed to keep faith with all future generations of this people. They in turn must keep His statutes as ordained in the Bible. The covenant is, however, unbreakable. They will be punished for their sins and judged by stricter standards than those God applies to other men, but He will never put them utterly aside and fine a new love.[31]

There is a Judaism founded on the temporary provisions of the Mosaic economy and the traditions of the past, which is irreconcilable with our doctrine of the Kingdom; and there is a Judaism grounded upon the Abrahamic and Davidic Covenants, and the promises to the nation, which is inseparably connected with our belief—indeed, is fundamental to it.[32]

The actual biblical covenants as given literally and inerrantly by God are the absolute essential foundation for an understanding of God's entire plan for mankind. Without this foundational cornerstone and basis for understanding and interpreting God's Word, overall interpretation becomes one of mere speculation and presumption.

---

[31] Arthur Hertzberg, ed., *Judaism* (New York: George Braziller, 1962), 11, 21, 22.
[32] Peters, *The Theocratic Kingdom*, 1:428.

God has literally put Himself under contract

The question we need to answer, what are the actual covenants that biblically define the fundamental foundation for God's massive kingdom program for mankind through the Jew, national Israel exclusively? The first and foundational covenant for all the other covenants is the Abrahamic covenant. This covenant is without doubt the most important covenant in Scripture as it lays the foundation for God's entire covenanted kingdom program. The Abrahamic, land, Davidic, and new covenants are the four biblical covenants that are eternal, unconditional, and unilateral and must be thoroughly comprehended to have any understanding of God's theocratic kingdom.

The land, Davidic, and new covenants are tied to and flow from the Abrahamic covenant. God by His sovereign choice has completely bound Himself to a biblically covenanted plan and program with the nation Israel. He has quite literally put Himself under contract to carry out His divine plan for the redemption of mankind, and the completed redemption from the curse. God's entire eschatological program is entirely spelled out in detail in these four biblical covenants. Dr. J. Dwight Pentecost comments:

> The covenants contained in the Scriptures are of primary importance to the interpreter of the Word and to the student of Eschatology. God's eschatological program is determined and prescribed by these covenants and one's eschatological system is determined and limited by the interpretation of them. These covenants must be studied diligently as the basis of Biblical Eschatology.[33]

---

[33] J. Dwight Pentecost, *Things to Come* (Grand Rapids: Zondervan, 1958), 65.

The only conclusive reason biblical pre-millennialism is valid is because it is entirely based and rooted in the complete truth of and reliance on the biblical covenants. This is the root and foundation to the complete eschatological program God has established and sworn by His very Person and Holiness. For this very reason it is impossible that He will change this course of action, it is virtually inviolable.[34] It is impossible for God to violate His own biblical covenants defining His own specific plan and purposes resulting ultimately in the rule of Christ in the theocratic or millennial kingdom. The Lord has literally and inerrantly spelled out in these biblical covenants exactly what He intends to do, and He has revealed this to man so he can understand His intended inviolable outcome.

If there were a possibility of any changes, there would be extensive and detailed revelation in the Text giving solid evidences that He has changed His plan. However, from Genesis to Revelation there is not the slightest hint that God has changed anything in His theocratic plan for the nation Israel.[35] Nothing can change the covenanted outcome, no man, no theology, not even Israel as a nation in its disobedience,[36] for

---

[34] See specifically Ps. 89; esp. vss. 33-37; 105; esp. 8-11; 132; esp. 10-18; Jer. 31:35-37; 33:14-26.

[35] The only changes are the ones man has made, and that is usually replacing Israel with the church, or other nations, or their own theology. Israel, the Jew in particular, is the master key for understanding God's entire Word for all the biblical covenants are effectively with the Jew. It must be remembered the whole Old Testament is really the history of the nation Israel (the Jews) and the coming of their biblically covenanted kingdom of God in Israel. Jesus will rule from the biblically defined Davidic throne in Jerusalem. How sad it is when men replace Israel and shift the Davidic throne to heaven. They play down God's covenanted program with Israel with something so foolish and inferior.

[36] The Lord even planned for Israel's disobedience in the biblical covenants. One example is in the Davidic covenant with David's seed or progeny. The Lord promised He would discipline David's seed as a son. "I will be a father to him and he will be a son to Me; when he commits iniquity, I will correct him with the rod of men and the strokes of the sons of men" (2 Sam. 7:14). This is repeated many times even in Psalms. "If his sons forsake My law, And do not walk in My judgments, If they violate My statutes, And do not

the biblical covenants are eternal, unilateral, and unconditional. God's plan and purposes are as immutable as He is (Mal. 3:6; Rom. 11:29) for they are contained in the biblical covenants spoken directly from Him and by Him. Every detail, every jot and tittle, must be executed flawlessly, for it is based on God's immutable character and Person. Alva J. McClain makes this comment:

> Through all the bitter prophecies of judgment uttered against Israel, there is never the slightest intimation that God's covenant with Israel can be broken or ultimately fail, but Jehovah never fails in His purpose: "For I am the Lord," He says, "I change not; therefore ye sons of Jacob are not consumed" (Mal. 3:6[37]).[38]

What made men such as C. I. Scofield, Alva J. McClain, Lewis Sperry Chafer, and others like these, especially George Peters[39] so mighty and confident in all their eschatological

---

keep My commandments, Then I will visit their transgression with the rod, And their iniquity with stripes" (Psalm 89:30-32). David himself was certainly disciplined as a son. But the Lord will never break His covenant with David. "Once I have sworn by My holiness; I will not lie to David" (Psalm 89:35).

[37] "For I, the LORD, do not change; therefore you, O sons of Jacob, are not consumed." Malachi 3:6 The basis of God's never destroying, deserting, or replacing Israel is realized in His inherent immutability. For I, the LORD, do not change (LXX) οὐκ ἠλλοίωμαι; כִּי אֲנִי יְהוָה לֹא שָׁנִיתִי; שָׁנָה *change.* "The verb is sometimes used to describe a change in character or way or life. Thus the immutability of God is expressed in Mal 3:6 by the statement that God does not change, and his faithfulness to his promise is shown in the statement that he will not alter that which he has spoken (Ps 89:34)" Harris, R. L., Archer, G. L., & Waltke, B. K., *Theological Wordbook of the Old Testament*, electronic ed. (Chicago: Moody Press, c1980, 1999). 941.

[38] Alva J. McClain, *The Greatness of the Kingdom* (Winona Lake: BMH Books, 1992), 119.

[39] George N. H. Peters, (1825-1909), born November 29, 1825 in New Berlin, Pennsylvania. He lived in Springfield, Ohio and attended Wittenberg College, a Lutheran school in Springfield. He pastored several Lutheran

dogma and doctrine, was a very deep understanding of the biblical covenants and what God has promised in these covenants to Israel. In George Peter's excellent work, *The Theocratic Kingdom,* he realized the basis of all biblical, systematic, and eschatological theology is in an understanding of the kingdom,[40] the theocratic kingdom, yet this was realized totally and exclusively from the biblical covenants. He among several other scholars believed that the kingdom must have the first place in all biblical and systematic theology.[41] This does not in any sense void Christ's work of redemption, and in fact enhances it. Peters addresses this very issue in *The Theocratic*

---

churches in Ohio. He did not agree with many of those in his denomination on issues of the kingdom for he was avidly premillennial in his eschatology, while his denomination was basically postmillennial. From his life's study of biblical prophecy emerged *The Theocratic Kingdom.*

[40] *"The Kingdom of God is a subject of vital importance.* The Scriptures cannot be rightly comprehended without a due knowledge of this kingdom. It is a fact, attested by a multitude of works, and constantly present in all phases of biblical literature, that the doctrine respecting the kingdom has materially affected the judgments of men concerning the canonical authority, the credibility, inspiration, and the meaning of the writers contained in the Bible. If in error here, it will inevitably manifest itself, e.g., in exegesis and criticism. This feature has been noticed by various writers, and, however explained, the views entertained on this subject are admitted to greatly modify the reception, the interpretation, and the doctrinal teaching of the Word." Peters, *The Theocratic Kingdom,* 1:30.

[41] "The kingdom deserves the first place in Biblical and the first rank in Systematic theology. The reasons for this, as already intimated, are abundant. This has been too much overlooked, and the kingdom has been placed in a subordinate position, until for some years past a reaction – induced by unbelieving attacks – has taken place, and the kingdom (however explained) is brought out again most prominently.... While thus advocating its claims to doctrinal position, we do not, as sometimes unjustly charged, depreciate the importance, the value, and the exceeding preciousness of the person and death of Jesus. The latter is doctrinally the outcome from the former, and as provisionary (for without the latter the kingdom, as covenanted and promised, could not possibly be obtained), for the kingdom is of incalculable consequence. If it be said that "the Christ" is of greater importance than the kingdom, this is fully admitted, inasmuch as the theocratic king who establishes the kingdom is greater than the kingdom itself." Peters, *The Theocratic Kingdom,* 1:30.

Kingdom in proposition one titled *The kingdom of God is a subject of vital importance.* He fully realized and acknowledged throughout his massive work and study that no one could come to an understanding of this kingdom program apart from a thorough comprehension of the biblical covenants. This is perfectly biblical as well as logical, for the biblical kingdom is derived exclusively from the biblical covenants as has been repeated over and over.

Peters continually references through thousands of pages of his monumental work[42] that Israel's biblical covenants are the foundation for God's entire redemptive kingdom program.

> The Kingdom anticipated *by the Jews at the First Advent is based on the Abrahamic and Davidic Covenants.* This might be shown by numerous references, but it will be sufficiently conspicuous by adverting to the declarations found in only one chapter of the New Testament. Thus, e.g., Luke 1:32, 33, 55, 72, 73, where we have undoubted allusions to previously obtained covenants, in the "mercy *promised* to the fathers," *in the "holy covenant"* confirmed by oath "to our father Abraham," and in "the throne of his father David." In turning back to the fountain head from whence this doctrine, this faith in Messianic Kingdom proceeds, we only reiterate what others have most aptly stated when we *invite for the covenants an absorbing interest in view of their living, fundamental connection with final salvation in Christ's Kingdom.* Kurtz (His. Old Cov., P.175) has well expressed this "*a foundation on which the great Salvation is ultimately to appear.*" Thorp (The Dest. Of the

---

[42] *The Theocratic Kingdom* …in this work Peters has recorded two hundred and six propositions all related exclusively to the kingdom of God. One would be very wise to look into some of his great work and genius. One might at least read the first proposition.

Brit. Empire, Pref. p. 8) justly observes: "*The
Abrahamic Covenant is the foundation of all the
dispensations of heaven, both to Jews and
Gentiles.*"[43]

Without this solid foundation, any theology is a rather
void and empty theology, especially when God's eschatological
program is so perfectly clear based on the biblical covenants.
While salvation or redemption is a main emphasis in Scripture,
this is not the *only* emphasis. If the biblical covenants are not
adhered to as a continuous guide of God's complete redemptive
program, then there will be no future and final redemptive
eschatological program for man especially the nation Israel on
this earth. The history of man and his final redemption as
presented in Scripture would be incomplete, as if God
undertook a plan and program with Adam (mankind) and was
not able to carry it out to its predetermined or predestined end.[44]
However, God has revealed His complete redemptive program
and kingdom and the many wonderful millennial prophecies
related to them.

These prophecies are directly related to the biblical
covenants. Both covenants and prophecies define the final
restoration[45] of man and the high calling he had when he was

---

[43] Ibid., 1:285.

[44]"For **the creation was subjected to futility**, not willingly, but because of
Him who subjected it, in hope that **the creation itself also will be set free
from its slavery to corruption into the freedom of the glory of the
children of God**. For we know that the whole creation groans and suffers the
pains of childbirth together until now" (Rom. 8:20-22); "And Jesus said to
them, Truly I say to you, that you who have followed Me, in the
regeneration when the Son of Man will sit on His glorious throne, you also
shall sit upon twelve thrones, judging the twelve tribes of Israel" (Mat.
19:28).

[45] Mankind, (Adam), created man, has never fulfilled what was originally
intended for him as man created in the image of God. Man was to rule and
have dominion over all things. The restoration of this image will be
completed in the Davidic Kingdom. "This Kingdom is a complete
restoration in the person of the Second Adam or Man, of the dominion lost
by the First Adam or Man.... The reign of Christ as the "Son of Man" points

originally created in the image of God.[46] Yet much more is at
stake here. Without a full understanding of the covenants as the
heart of this whole matter, there is no possibility for a thorough
and complete interpretation of *all* Scripture. Covenants are the
floodgate upon which inerrant and progressive truth is based.
Jots and tittles are flawlessly and inerrantly in place and reveal
His covenanted kingdom program.

There is much more to be gleaned from the truth God
has posited in Scripture as the basis of His entire kingdom
program than simply redemptive or even Christological. His
ultimate purpose is always doxological and this cannot be
whittle down to one component of His Word.. Whether
Christological, salvific, redemptive, theocratic, etc. or even
allowing the fall, He will always bring glory to Himself. He is
sovereign in all He does and deserves all the glory.

In His divine plan He has spelled out His kingdom
program by precise words of biblical covenants that
communicate literal truth culminating in a literal redemptive

---

us back to the fall in which humanity was so sadly involved, and then
forward to the period when humanity, through this manifestation of this Son
of Man, is fully restored to the blessings forfeited by the fall. Among these
blessings a right royal one is grounded in the developing Plan of
Redemption, by which man shall again be restored to the dignity of
dominion through Him, who by virtue of His relationship to the human in the
covenanted line, has obtained the forfeited right originally granted to man,
and which, as King on David's throne, will be most gloriously exerted, being
sublimely and irresistibly aided by the Divine united with Him.... Peters,
The Theocratic Kingdom, 1:572.

[46]"What the Roman Catholic writer, Schlegel (Phil. Of His., s. 1), says, in
opposition to the idea of man's low origin, we, in view of the Divine unity of
Purpose thus manifested, can repeat: "We may boldly answer, that, man on
the contrary, was originally, and by the very constitution of his being,
designed to be lord of creation, and, though in a subordinate degree, the
legitimate ruler of the earth and the world around him; the vicegerent of God
in nature." God will not allow sin to triumph in the utter destruction of this
grant, but will evince that grace in Jesus, the Christ, that will secure the
victory in this as well as in all other respects. Tholuck (com. Rom. 5:12)
produces a Jewish Rabbi, who remarks: "The secret of Adam is the secret of
the Messiah." "As the first man was the one that sinned, so shall the Messiah
be the one to do sin away. Peters, *The Theocratic Kingdom*, 1:575-576.

earthly kingdom and throne. There is then something vitally essential to God's program that is fundamentally connected with so great a salvation springing forth from His biblical covenants. Man will be redeemed and restored to the great calling in which he was originally created as the son of God[47] by the Son of God[48] to a perfect and completed redemption from the curse.[49] The biblical covenants must be totally accepted, understood, and studied to comprehend any of this.

---

[47]**Note the Luke three genealogy:** "When He began His ministry, Jesus Himself was about thirty years of age, being, as was supposed, the son of Joseph, the son of Eli...the son of David, the son of Jesse, the son of Obed, the son of Boaz, the son of Salmon, the son of Nahshon, the son of Amminadab, the son of Admin, the son of Ram, the son of Hezron, the son of Perez, the son of Judah, the son of Jacob, the son of Isaac, the son of Abraham, the son of Terah, the son of Nahor, the son of Serug, the son of Reu, the son of Peleg, the son of Heber, the son of Shelah, the son of Cainan, the son of Arphaxad, the son of Shem, the son of Noah, the son of Lamech, the son of Methuselah, the son of Enoch, the son of Jared, the son of Mahalaleel, the son of Cainan, the son of Enosh, the son of Seth, the **son of Adam, the son of God**" (Luke 3:23-38). The 'article' is denoting the relationship at creation... "τοῦ Ἐνὼς τοῦ Σὴθ **τοῦ Ἀδὰμ τοῦ θεοῦ.**" (Luke 3:38).

[48]"O Lord, our Lord, How majestic is Your name in all the earth, Who have displayed Your splendor above the heavens! From the mouth of infants and nursing babes You have established strength Because of Your adversaries, To make the enemy and the revengeful cease. When I consider Your heavens, the work of Your fingers, The moon and the stars, which You have ordained; **What is man that You take thought of him, And the son of man that You care for him? Yet You have made him a little lower than God, And You crown him with glory and majesty! You make him to rule over the works of Your hands; You have put all things under his feet, All sheep and oxen, And also the beasts of the field, The birds of the heavens and the fish of the sea, Whatever passes through the paths of the seas.** O Lord, our Lord, How majestic is Your name in all the earth!" (Psalm 8); "You have put all things in subjection under his feet. For in subjecting all things to him, **He left nothing that is not subject to him. But now we do not yet see all things subjected to him. But we do see Him who was made for a little while lower than the angels, namely, Jesus, because of the suffering of death crowned with glory and honor, so that by the grace of God He might taste death for everyone**"(Hebr. 2:8-9).

[49] In the covenanted millennial kingdom one curse will not be lifted: "The wolf and the lamb will graze together, and the lion will eat straw like the ox;

One must be a student of the biblical covenants

If one is a student of the Word, he must be a student of the biblical covenants. Covenant theologians are truly students of covenants, but they are the wrong covenants. Their covenants are manmade and this is one of the main reasons for various forms of replacement theology and/or preterism. Covenant theology is based on an entire system on one, two, or three covenants that simply don't exist. It is strange how they assail a consistent literal interpretation which leads to His kingdom.

Most all prophecy flows from the promises of the biblical covenants made exclusively with the nation Israel. Although a certain portion of biblical prophecy may be fulfilled, there is a vast distinction between fulfilled biblical prophecy and fulfilled biblical covenant promises.

Covenant theology which usually redefines or replaces Israel with the church,[50] is virtually inconceivable if the biblical covenants are adhered to as inerrantly foundational to God's entire revealed program. To pay little heed to them is convenient for a manmade or conceived theological system, but it is hardly biblical scholarship and grossly presumptuous when approaching the great truths of God's Word.

While any theology may claim that covenants are its true foundation, there is no possibility they can be violated without doing damage to the entire structure of that system. It is also inconceivable to have a theological system that is biblical not be based on the root[51] of the biblical covenants. Progressive

---

and dust will be the serpent's food. They will do no evil or harm in all My holy mountain, says the Lord" (Isaiah 65:25).

[50]This would include any form of a similar replacement theology or even preterism. There are variations of replacement theology.

[51] In Rom. 11:17-25 Paul gave severe warning to those Gentiles in Rome who appeared to be arrogant to the nation Israel. This may have been a beginning of 'replacement theology.' Gentiles are the wild or unnatural branch and Israel is the natural branch i.e. natural in relation to all the promises of the biblical covenants. Israel has been 'set aside' for a season so salvation may come to the Gentiles until the fullness of the Gentiles come in. The root supporting Israel is only one thing biblically 'the great promises in

dispensationalism which is not dispensationalism in any sense simply does not have the biblical covenants as its foundation. If this were true, all one would hear is the literal reestablishment of the literal kingdom to Israel in the literal land, the literal earthly Davidic throne, not some kingdom now or throne in heaven. The biblical covenants simply won't allow any such interpretation. Ultimately God's revelation and eschatological program is literally and inerrantly spelled out in the God and blood ordained biblical covenants (Gen. 15:8-12; Luke 22:20; 1 Cor. 11:25; Heb. 9:15-22).

> Indeed it is universally admitted, however explained afterward, that the covenants are the proper basis of future Revelation, and that they contain in an epitomized form *the substance* of God's Purpose in reference to man's Salvation,

---

the covenants, especially the Abrahamic covenant. The covenants literally define the nation Israel and all the promises that must be fulfilled. "I say then, they did not stumble so as to fall, did they? May it never be! But by their transgression **salvation has come to the Gentiles, to make them jealous**. Now if their transgression is riches for the world and their failure is riches for the Gentiles, how much more will their fulfillment be! But I am speaking to you who are Gentiles. Inasmuch then as I am an apostle of Gentiles, I magnify my ministry, if somehow I might move to jealousy my fellow countrymen and save some of them. **For if their rejection is the reconciliation of the world, what will their acceptance be but life from the dead**? If the first piece of dough is holy, the lump is also; and if the root is holy, the branches are too. But if some of the branches were broken off, and you, being a wild olive, were grafted in among them and became partaker with them of the rich root of the olive tree, do not be arrogant toward the branches; but if you are arrogant, **remember that it is not you who supports the root, but the root supports you**" (Rom. 11:11-18). Even though the root 'supports the Gentiles' in that they are heirs also by their relationship by faith to Christ, there is great warning to those who believe any Gentiles or the church in any sense has replaced Israel with all the biblically covenanted promises. "You will say then, Branches were broken off so that I might be grafted in. Quite right, they were broken off for their unbelief, but you stand by your faith. Do not be conceited, but fear; **for if God did not spare the natural branches, He will not spare you, either**" (Rom. 11:19-21).

the Messiah's Kingdom and glory, and the perfected Redemption from the curse. Hence, men of all shades of opinion agreeing in this matter, it is essential for any one who desires to become *a real student* of God's Word to make himself familiar with these covenants, seeing, that, in the nature of the case, all things following must correspond fully with these previously given pledges and guides. While the covenants are necessarily *primary* in a proper conception of the Divine Plan relating to Redemption, presenting a *central idea*, the reader will observe that they are scripturally based and grammatically founded on *direct oath-bound promises,* and hence are to be distinguished from that vague scholastic mystical effort to make the covenants a central idea as given e.g. by John Cocceisus... and others. This grasping after the covenants as a foundation thought relating to the Kingdom of Christ is characteristic of the German Reformed ... and is found in theologians of ability in various denominations. Unfortunately, however, many have *much to say* about a covenant made between the Father and Son in eternity – of which we have no record, and which opens a door for conjecture and unproven inferences – while they *ignore*, more or less, those on record.[52]

It seems many people today neither understand the biblical covenants with Israel thoroughly nor even want to. What makes George Peters and men like him such giants in the theology of God's eschatological program especially that of *The Theocratic Kingdom* is this tremendous knowledge of the biblical covenants. Peters was talking of this lack of knowledge

---

[52] Peters, *The Theocratic Kingdom*, 1:285.

of the covenants over 150 years ago. Theologians such as Peters, Chafer, Scofield, and McClain understood that any position that *violates* the God given biblical covenants made by sovereign decree is a direct assault against promises God had sworn to accomplish by His own Person and Holiness[53] with Israel. This idea is often missing from the majority of bible teaching as one reads and studies various systematic theologies.

Conclusion

In the church there is very little understanding of the biblical covenants[54] of His inerrant Word. They truly define His entire redemptive kingdom program with all men.

---

[53] "But I will not break off My lovingkindness from him, Nor deal falsely in My faithfulness. My covenant I will not violate, Nor will I alter the utterance of My lips. **Once I have sworn by My holiness**; I will not lie to David. His descendants shall endure forever, and his throne as the sun before Me. It shall be established forever like the moon, and the witness in the sky is faithful" (Psalm 89:33-37).

[54] As an example: In the church there are normally two biblical ordinances, baptism and communion, where the latter involves His body (substitution) and His blood of the new covenant (1 Cor. 11:24-25). "And when He had given thanks, He broke it, and said, this is My body, which is for you; do this in remembrance of Me." In the same way *He took* the cup also, after supper, saying, this cup is the new covenant in My blood; do this, as often as you drink *it*, in remembrance of Me" (1 Cor. 11:24-25). ὡσαύτως καὶ τὸ ποτήριον μετὰ τὸ δειπνῆσαι λέγων· τοῦτο τὸ ποτήριον **ἡ καινὴ διαθήκη ἐστὶν** ἐν τῷ ἐμῷ αἵματι· τοῦτο ποιεῖτε, ὁσάκις ἐὰν πίνητε, εἰς τὴν ἐμὴν ἀνάμνησιν (1 Corinthians 11:25). The average church or church member usually has very little understanding as to what the blood of the new covenant refers. They are actually celebrating His blood redemption of the new covenant, no fulfillment for the church, but they do this in remembrance of Him until He comes. This covenant is made with Israel and can only be fulfilled by God in Israel. This is sad in the light of the context of the judgments that were being poured out on the Corinthians (1 Cor. 11:17-34; esp. 27) in relation to the new covenant while in no way fulfilling the new covenant. The cup τὸ ποτήριον... ἐν τῷ ἐμῷ αἵματι has to be explained as that being representative of the new covenant; ἡ καινὴ διαθήκη not '*a* new

The biblical covenants might be much more serious business than the student of Scripture might realize. Great prudence should be exercised in light of many cavalier interpretations relating to biblical covenants especially those involving any kind of preterism or replacement theology. The key to understanding God's entire kingdom program is the biblical covenants.

---

covenant' but ἡ καινὴ διαθήκη something Paul and the Corinthians fully understood and were being reprimanded for not handling properly.

Chapter 8
God's Covenanted His Kingdom with David

The importance of the Davidic covenant

No other covenant of all the biblical covenants is more important than the Davidic covenant in defining the Lord's covenanted throne and kingdom. God's covenanted theocratic kingdom program is completely identified with David's throne and kingdom. The Davidic covenant establishes David's seed who must literally descend from the lineage of David, and who must literally reign from David's throne over David's kingdom. This covenant establishes David's house, David's throne, and David's kingdom. This in itself demonstrates the great importance and very essence of the Davidic covenant. "When your days are complete and you lie down with your fathers, I will raise up **your descendant** after you, who will come forth from you, and I will establish his **kingdom**. He shall build a house for My name, and I will establish **the throne** of his kingdom **forever**. I will be a father to him and he will be a son to Me; when he commits iniquity, I will correct him with the rod of men and the strokes of the sons of men, but My lovingkindness shall not depart from him, as I took it away from Saul, whom I removed from before you. And **your house and your kingdom** shall endure before Me **forever**; **your throne** shall be established **forever**." (2 Sam. 7:12-16)[1]

God had already established that there would be kings or a kingly line coming from the Abrahamic seed line (Gen.

---

[1] Observe carefully the promise of *the house, kingdom, and throne*, with the emphasis on the *throne of the kingdom* (Solomon's) being established *forever*, and David's *throne* being established *forever*. To confuse David's throne, kingdom, Solomon's throne, and kingdom (identical thrones and kingdom) for some other eternal or heavenly throne and kingdom, is to purposely avoid the promises of the Davidic covenant. If there is another throne and kingdom with David, Scripture speaks nothing of it, and it is of very trivial concern, unless one wishes to violate this covenant for another theology.

17:6).[2] This line was identified with Jacob (Gen. 35:10-12),[3] and then Judah (Gen. 49:10-12),[4] but the continuation and details of the kingly line and the kingdom was not established and fully covenanted until David (2 Sam. 7:12-16). This is why it is essential to understand the importance and significance of the Davidic covenant which truly defines God's covenanted kingdom program. This covenant not only defines the throne and kingdom of David but all the essential details of the seed line. This is vital as to who inherits the Davidic throne and kingdom.

---

[2] The first promise of kings to Abraham was later in Genesis 17:6. While the first promises to Abraham of the covenant are in Genesis 12:1-3, the covenant is expanded later, especially with the promise of kings to Abraham. *"And I will make you exceedingly fruitful, and I will make nations of you,* **and kings shall come forth from you** וּמְלָכִים מִמְּךָ יֵצֵאוּ (Genesis 17:6). God was very clear that kings would come forth from Abraham. This promise will be very much carried through to Judah (Gen. 49:10-12) and then to the Davidic covenant.

[3] "And God said to him, "Your name is Jacob; you shall no longer be called Jacob, But Israel shall be your name." Thus, He called him Israel. God also said to him, "I am God Almighty; be fruitful and multiply; A nation and a company of nations shall come from you, **and kings shall come forth from you** וּמְלָכִים מֵחֲלָצֶיךָ יֵצֵאוּ. "And the land which I gave to Abraham and Isaac, I will give it to you, and I will give the land to your descendants after you."" (Genesis 35:10-12). Everything is being promised to Jacob, including the land promises. But the promise of kings is made to Jacob also. It was important to repeat this from the original promise of kings to Abraham as the promised line of kings is now Abraham, Isaac, and now repeated to Jacob (Israel). Up to now there were no kings from them in the promised kingly line.

[4] The promised rule, seed line of rule or kingly line, must come through Judah. This is made very clear in these verses. Kings have already been promised for Israel, and Judah will play a significant part in the seed line. "**The scepter** shall not depart from Judah, Nor the ruler's staff from between his feet, Until Shiloh comes, And to him shall be the obedience of the peoples. "He ties his foal to the vine, And his donkey's colt to the choice vine; He washes his garments in wine, And his robes in the blood of grapes. "His eyes are dull from wine, And his teeth white from milk." (Genesis 49:10-12).

Saul was not God's choice

In the history of the kings of Israel, it was obvious that Saul was not God's choice as king for this was the will of the people.[5] God had already planned to establish a kingdom with a king, as kings were already promised to Abraham in the Abrahamic covenant (Gen. 17:6). This kingly rule or seed line was established by prophecy already through the tribe of Judah not through the tribe Benjamin (Saul). "The scepter shall not depart from Judah, nor the ruler's staff from between his feet, Until Shiloh[6] comes, and to him shall be the obedience of the peoples" (Gen. 49:10). This is a most remarkable prophecy especially referring to the one who is coming, and "to him shall be the obedience of the peoples." If the kings came directly through Jacob with no other explanation or prophecy, then there would be no need for a further detailed lineage of kings or rulers. This makes it quite clear that the kingly line must come through Judah. The Davidic covenant established the royal seed line of Davidic kings, which will culminate in the final seed,

---

[5]The Lord יְהֹוָה is always the sovereign King over His creation. No man is given this rule especially from heaven. The definition of a theocracy is 'a form of government where God is recognized as the supreme Ruler.' By Israel asking for a king to rule over them as the other nations, they were essentially rejecting the rule of God over them, or a true theocracy (1 Sam. 8:4-8).

[6] "In this oracle, Jacob predicted a fierce lionlike dominance of Judah over his enemies and over his brothers who would praise him. A wordplay was made here on the name Judah which means "praise" ..... The oracle pivots on the word until (49:10b). When the Promised One who will rule the nations appears, the scene will become an earthly paradise. These verses anticipate the kingship in Judah culminating in the reign of Messiah (cf. the tribe of Judah, Rev. 5:5), in which nations will obey Him. The NASB renders the third line of Genesis 49:10, "Until Shiloh comes." Many sources, including the Targum (Aramaic paraphrase of the OT), see "Shiloh" as a title of the Messiah. However, the Hebrew word šîlōh should be rendered "whose it is," that is, the scepter will not depart from Judah . . . until He comes whose it (i.e., the scepter) is (or as the NIV puts it, to whom it belongs)." Allen P Ross, "Genesis," in *The Bible knowledge commentary, Old Testament,* ed. John F. Walvoord and Roy B. Zuck (Wheaton, Ill.: Victor, 1983), 98-99.

God's anointed, or the Lord's Messiah. God has fully established 'the Christ' by covenant design. Jesus is the 'Christ' who is Heir Apparent to the Davidic throne and kingdom.

By Israel's selection of Saul or effectively any king, the nation actually displayed a willful ignorance or disdain for God's kingdom program having been already rooted in the Abrahamic covenant. For the rule of God over Israel must be accepted as effectively lodged in the Abrahamic covenant, or else it would be needless to say "but they have rejected Me from being king over them" (1 Sam. 8:7). There are several reasons for this, which are most important to understand.

At the time of the selection of Saul by the people, there was no biblical covenant concerning Israel that promised a designated kingly or messianic line and throne as the Davidic covenant. There would be no other reason to have the promise of kings and establish a kingly line unless for the establishment of a kingdom with Israel, and this proves even more that the kingdom program was rooted in the Abrahamic covenant (Gen. 17:6; 35:11). This is definitely born out with the selection of Saul by the people, as they should have known; God had already promised kings by covenant decree. The Lord being the sovereign King or Theocratic King of the universal kingdom would eventually provide the covenanted kingly line and king. By rejecting His choice of kings, which were already promised by covenant design and specifically through Judah (Gen. 49:10-12), Israel displayed the willful rejection of the Lord as their King. "And the Lord said to Samuel, listen to the voice of the people in regard to all that they say to you, for they have not rejected you, but they have rejected Me from being king over them" (1 Samuel 8:7).[7] All this would prove to be most

---

[7]"They wanted a king, because they imagined that Jehovah their God-king was not able to secure their constant prosperity. Instead of seeking for the cause of the misfortunes which had hitherto befallen them in their own sin and want of fidelity towards Jehovah, they searched for it in the faulty constitution of the nation itself." C. F. Keil & F. Delitzsch, *Commentary on the Old Testament*, 10 vols. (Peabody: Hendrickson, 1996 reprint), 2:419. It

significant especially when the Lord would eventually establish the promised seed line for His earthly throne and kingdom with David rooted completely in the Davidic covenant.

The covenanted Davidic progeny

The covenanted kingdom and throne are fully established in the seed of David by the Davidic covenant (2 Sam. 7:12-15). Note the promises in the Davidic covenant especially related to David's seed or son. The emphasis of this covenant is mostly concerning David's son.

1. When your days are complete, David dies
2. I will raise up **your descendant**, *David's son*
3. I will establish **his kingdom,** *David's son*
4. He shall build a house for My name, *David's son*
5. I will establish **the throne of his kingdom forever**, *David's son*
6. I will be a father to him and he will be a son to Me, *David's son*
7. When he commits iniquity, I will correct him, *David's son*
8. But My lovingkindness shall not depart from him, *David's son*
9. **Your house & your kingdom** shall endure before Me **forever,** David
10. **Your throne** shall be established **forever,** David

---

is important to note Saul's later response: "But you today rejected your God, who delivers you from all your calamities and your distresses; yet you have said, 'No, but set a king over us!' Now therefore, present yourselves before the Lord by your tribes and by your clans" (1 Samuel 10:19). Even from the beginning God will always be Israel's true King even in the millennium (Zech. 14:9). Jesus as the God-man in the kingdom will be recognized as not only the true covenanted king of Israel, but also the Divine king. "And the Lord will be king over all the earth; in that day the Lord will be the only one, and His name the only one" (Zechariah 14:9).

For a complete understanding of the kingdom, the throne of David, the throne of his son, etc. a comprehensive study of this covenant and all the details that are in it are mandatory. For without the Davidic covenant and a systematic understanding of it in relation to the other eternal covenants, there is no defined seed, no defined throne, no defined kingdom, no defined house (dynasty), and no defined Davidic progeny to inherit the covenanted throne and kingdom of David. If this covenant is not fully embraced, the definition of the Davidic throne and kingdom would be left in the hands of anyone who wishes to redefine what God has promised and covenanted with David through his Son.

The very words of this covenant establish the Davidic throne and kingdom as well as his son's, which is the same throne and kingdom. No other Text redefines this coming kingdom program. One very powerful reason for this is that God has taken oaths that He will fulfill what He had promised to David and his son (Ps. 89:3-4; 33-37; 105:8-11; 132:10-12). God has sealed these covenants ultimately with His Son's own blood. It is essential to understand how the complete establishment of God's kingdom program with David as specifically covenanted is the vital key to understanding all future prophecy and promises related to it.

Prophecy, as given in Scriptures of itself, does not establish the eternal kingdom program of God. The entire redemptive kingdom program[8] was founded only upon the

---

[8] It must be continually kept in focus that only the redeemed or regenerate will enter His coming kingdom. He taught this very specifically to Nicodemus. "Now there was a man of the Pharisees, named Nicodemus, a ruler of the Jews; this man came to Him by night, and said to Him, Rabbi, we know that You have come from God *as* a teacher; for no one can do these signs that You do unless God is with him. Jesus answered and said to him, truly, truly, I say to you, **unless one is born again, he cannot see the kingdom of God.** Nicodemus said to Him, How can a man be born when he is old? He cannot enter a second time into his mother's womb and be born, can he? Jesus answered, truly, truly, I say to you, unless one is **born of water and the Spirit, he cannot enter into the kingdom of God.** That

biblical covenants. What establishes the entire redemptive program and the defining of the throne and the kingdom God are the eternal covenants themselves and nothing else. In addition, all biblical prophecy ultimately flows from the biblical covenants. The prophets and the prophecies are progressively displaying God's continued development toward His covenanted kingdom program and its final phase. This would be Jesus the Christ,[9] David's ultimate son, ruling as the Messiah i.e. the Christ from David's covenanted throne over David's kingdom. This is what the Scriptures are revealing, and it is important to realize the progression that God has given in His Word by revelation through prophecy toward this kingdom. Peters comments on the lack of focus by the church of His covenanted kingdom:

> It is significant to the thoughtful student – a fulfillment of prophecy – that the idea of a distinctive Divine kingdom related to Christ and this earth, a kingdom which decidedly holds the foremost place in the teaching of Jesus, should be made, both (with few exceptions) in theology and the confessions of the Church, to come down from its first position in the Bible and occupy, when alluded to, *a very subordinate one*. In hundreds of books, where it reasonably ought to be conspicuous, a few references of a somewhat

---

which is born of the flesh is flesh, and that which is born of the Spirit is spirit. Do not marvel that I said to you, 'You must be born again" (John 3:1-7). One always had to be born from above to go to heaven. Jesus is speaking here of His coming kingdom *not heaven*. Only the redeemed will enter His earthly kingdom or millennial reign. This is why His kingdom might be referred to as the redemptive kingdom.

[9]"Whoever believes that **Jesus is the Christ** is born of God; and whoever loves the Father loves the *child* born of Him" (1 John 5:1). It is very strange how many say they believe in Jesus Christ without the understanding that He is the Christ in the biblical sense of what is being discussed concerning the covenants and His kingdom.

mystical and unsatisfactory nature, or a brief
endorsement of the old monkish view that it
applies to the Church, dismisses the entire
subject; while inferior subjects have long
chapters and even volumes in their interest.
There is, to the reflecting mind, something
radically wrong in such a change of position, and
the wider the departure from the scriptural basis
the more defective does it become. Any effort,
as here made, to restore the doctrine of the
kingdom to its true and paramount Biblical
station should at least solicit attention.[10]

The Scriptures reveal a theology of God's covenanted
Messianic kingdom with Israel in the covenanted land. This is
why the first promise addressed in the Abrahamic covenant was
'the land.' Kings were promised in the Abrahamic covenant.
Christ taught His disciples to seek His kingdom above all else
and pray for its coming. The actual charge at Christ's
crucifixion was that He was King of the Jews. There is much
more to this that will be addressed. (*See the chapter on the
nature of His kingdom*)

God's Anointed will ultimately rule from the Davidic
throne of His father's defined and covenanted kingdom.[11] The
issue is what throne and kingdom are the covenants and
prophecies actually describing. The church age has produced
many theories i.e. literally a virtual plethora of thrones and
kingdoms. There is as many hypothetical thrones and kingdoms
as there is sand on the beach. If one does not hold to the
absolute integrity of the eternal biblical covenants by definition,
then any conjured up throne and kingdom will be on sinking
sand. John the Baptist, Jesus, His disciples were only
concerned with the covenanted throne and kingdom.

---

[10] George N. H. Peters, The Theocratic Kingdom, 3 vols. (Grand Rapids:
Kregel, 1988 reprint), 1:31.
[11] What man did not do in Adam, the last Adam will fulfill what man was to
do under God's love and care.

Without the Davidic covenant there is no kingdom and no King

It is vital to understand the absolute necessity of a complete comprehension of the certain and fixed promises made to David and his seed or son in the Davidic covenant concerning God's kingdom program. For without the Davidic covenant, nothing is absolute concerning the seed, the house, the throne, the kingdom or the dynasty of David. The throne and the kingdom itself could not be established by anyone. Even the Messiah could not be properly identified as the One who must reign from David's throne. Without the Davidic covenant, there is nothing defined and nothing is established in relation to the throne and the kingdom of David.

Therefore, if nothing were defined regarding the seed of David or his kingdom promised in the Davidic covenant, then what the angel Gabriel said to Mary at the annunciation would have virtually no meaning. "And behold, you will conceive in your womb, and bear a son, and you shall name Him **Jesus.** He will be great, and will be called the Son of the Most High; and the Lord God will give Him **the throne of His father David;** and He will reign over **the house of Jacob forever**; and **His kingdom will have no end**" (Luke 1:31-33).[12] The throne of the kingdom of David referred to by Gabriel, which would be given to the child in Mary's womb, must be the same as that of His father David which was an eternal kingdom not 'a church'. Moreover, that eternal throne is known only from the Davidic covenant. There would be no Jew, including Mary, who would

---

[12]This is a very powerful passage in light of the Davidic covenant. The throne of David is only that which was known as that one David occupied and his son Solomon and his sons. David is called the father of Jesus as he is the true father through whom Christ, the anointed, inherits David's throne, so it can be literally said 'the Lord God will give to Him the throne of His father David' (Luke 1:32-33). If one takes the Text literally then this is not a heavenly throne in any sense. It is amazing how many have bought into such sad exegesis under the guise of scholarship.

have understood what was being said if the Davidic covenant were not taken literally and in effect.

Paul's *magnum opus*, the epistle to the Romans, would have no validity if the Davidic covenant were not comprehended literally. Paul reminds the Romans that Christ Jesus is the eternal Son born a descendant of David. "Paul, a bond-servant of Christ Jesus, called as an apostle, set apart for the gospel of God, which He promised beforehand through His prophets in the holy Scriptures, concerning His Son, who **was born of a descendant of David** [13] **according to the flesh**, who was declared **the Son of God** with power by the resurrection from the dead, according to the Spirit of holiness, Jesus Christ our Lord" (Romans 1:1-4).

Even the Pharisees knew full well that the Christ was a son of David. This son must be in the proper lineage of David to be the Christ. They had all the genealogies at that time and there was never a real challenge that Jesus was not in the proper lineage.

Most in Israel also understood that the Christ was a son of David. "Then there was brought to Him a demon-possessed man *who was* blind and dumb, and He healed him, so that the dumb man spoke and saw. And all the multitudes were amazed, and *began* to say, this *man* cannot be the Son of David, can he?" (Mat. 12:22-23). The adverb for 'cannot' in Greek usually requires a negative response. But it can also be used to indicate

---

[13] This is quite descript as Jesus must be from the literal seed of David. Again, this is quite descript, and it needs to be for covenanted defined reasons especially to be the proper seed of David. Paul places this very first in the book of Romans. This is most significant as Paul is using the Davidic seed connection to the Davidic covenant to prove the outworking of God's program especially through the nation Israel. If the Davidic covenant was still valid in the first century, it still is now. That covenant is very much in effect for everything promised to David must be fulfilled. God's entire program is based on it, and God's very holiness (character) is at stake (Ps. 89:33-37). Christ must be in this covenanted seed line to be the Christ, the ultimate descendant of David to whom all the promises are ultimately fulfilled. Without the Davidic covenant there is no seed line of the Messiah Who will rule over Israel on David's throne.

that the questioner is in doubt regarding the answer. No matter what, the multitudes were questioning whether this is 'the Son of David.'

The leadership of Israel was challenged and directed to the sonship issue by Jesus Himself. "Now while the Pharisees were gathered together, Jesus asked them a question, saying, what do you think about the Christ, whose son is He? **they said to Him, the son of David**. He said to them, Then how does David in the Spirit call Him 'Lord,' saying, The Lord said to my Lord, Sit at My right hand, Until I put Thine enemies beneath Thy feet" (Mat. 22:41-44). However, Jesus answers them with this statement. "If David then calls Him 'Lord,' how is He his son?" (Mat. 22:45). The challenge was that surrounding David's son. "Christ was trying to make the Pharisees see that the Son of David was also the Lord of David (Ps. 110:1); i.e., the Messiah was David's human descendant and Divine Lord."[14] "Psalm 110:1 uses two different Hebrew words for God. The first, translated Lord, is the name Yahweh, the proper name of Israel's God. The second Lord means "Master." David, the great king of Israel, calls one of his offspring "Lord" or "Master," a title for deity. The implication is that Jesus, the Son of David, is God. He is a descendant of David and therefore human, but He is also divine."[15]

The Christ is truly the God-man, but the Christ must come in David's royal seed line. The Pharisees and all Israel could only understand this from the Davidic covenant if taken literally for Jesus asked them what they thought about the Christ, whose son is He?

If Jesus were not the descendant of David and Heir according to the flesh, the Messiah of Israel to rule from David's throne, there is no gospel. Remember this is a redemptive-kingdom as such for only the redeemed may enter His kingdom (John 3:1-5). The Messiah is the God-man, that

---

[14] Charles C. Ryrie, *The Ryrie Study Bible* (Chicago: Moody, 1978), 1486.
[15] Earl D. Radmacher, gen. ed., *The Nelson Study Bible* (Nashville: Thomas Nelson, 1997), 1618.

is, He is fully God and fully man, but man according to the flesh of the seed of David. Matthew begins his gospel with this fact, and Paul begins Romans with this fact. This also shows the absolute necessity and literalness of the Davidic covenant.

The biblical covenants prove and articulate one kingdom

"Now in those days John the Baptist came, preaching in the wilderness of Judea, saying, repent, for the kingdom of heaven is at hand" (Mat. 3:1-2). When John announced the kingdom was at hand, he was announcing the coming Davidic kingdom. The eternal biblical covenants defined this kingdom of heaven. Notice there was no explanation of the throne and kingdom given by anyone. It was not necessary as Israel understood there would be coming the covenanted kingdom for them (Luke 2:25; 36-38; Act. 1:6). Israel was and is still God's elect and covenanted people and nation for this very purpose (Deut. 7:6-8; Ezek. 43:7).

John the baptizer, Jesus, the disciples only presented one kingdom. They all proclaimed, preached, and taught the same coming kingdom. There were not and are not multiple kingdoms. John was announcing the covenanted Davidic kingdom and Jesus as the Christ (Anointed, Messiah) of this kingdom. The gospel[16] of God, the kingdom of God and the kingdom of heaven were identical messages as they represented the coming kingdom message.

These expressions are totally interchangeable for there was only one coming kingdom covenanted in the Text. This is the only kingdom Christ and the disciples proclaimed and taught. While the kingdom was at hand or near, no one preached that the kingdom had come in the sense it already started for this is not possible. No one not even Paul taught an

---

[16] This is simply the gospel or 'the good news' from God concerning His kingdom. One still had to be born again to go into His kingdom (John 3:1-7).

already present kingdom.[17] John announced the coming King and kingdom for the kingdom was near but never here until Israel accepted the truth of their Davidic King. He is King of the Jews and they did not want Him as their King. There is no kingdom until they do.

Note well John the Baptist, Jesus, and his disciples were all preaching and proclaiming the same kingdom. There were not two separate gospels, two or more separate kingdoms; they were preaching the gospel or good news of the King and His kingdom. There seems to be so much confusion concerning this issue, and it is really quite easy if one believes in one covenanted kingdom being presented in the Text. If not, then there are multiple kingdoms with multiple thrones with multiple gospels.

The kingdom of heaven and the kingdom of God are identical

There is so much confusion concerning the kingdom of God, the kingdom of heaven, the gospel of the kingdom, etc. that it is necessary to show they are all identical expressions. They are all interchangeable as can be easily observed.

John presented the gospel of the coming King and kingdom to Israel. Note well *all* the expressions used by John, Jesus, and His disciples concerning this coming kingdom.

John the Baptist preached one kingdom

"Now in those days John the Baptist came, preaching in the wilderness of Judea, saying, Repent, for the **kingdom of heaven** is at hand" (Mat. 3:1-2).

"The Law and the Prophets *were proclaimed* until John; since then **the gospel of the kingdom of God** is preached, and everyone is forcing his way into it" (Luke 16:16).

---

[17]Paul preached a message of a coming kingdom to the church. "And he stayed two full years in his own rented quarters, and was welcoming all who came to him, **preaching the kingdom of God**, and teaching concerning the Lord Jesus Christ with all openness, unhindered" (Acts 28:30-31).

John did not present two separate kingdoms. The kingdom of heaven and the kingdom of God are identical.

Jesus presented the same kingdom with the same expressions. Jesus presented the gospel of His kingdom which was near and being offered to His covenant people, Israel. This was the good news of His kingdom.

Jesus preached and taught one kingdom

"From that time **Jesus** began to preach and say, Repent, for the **kingdom of heaven** is at hand" (Mat. 4:17).

"And **Jesus** was going about all the cities and the villages, teaching in their synagogues, and proclaiming **the gospel of the kingdom**, and healing every kind of disease and every kind of sickness" (Mat. 9:35).

"And after John had been taken into custody, **Jesus** came into Galilee, **preaching the gospel of God**, and saying, The time is fulfilled, and **the kingdom of God** is at hand; repent and **believe in the gospel**" (Mark 1:14-15).

"But when **Jesus** saw this, He was indignant and said to them, Permit the children to come to Me; do not hinder them; for **the kingdom of God** belongs to such as these" (Mark 10:14).

"But He said to them, I must preach the **kingdom of God** to the other cities also, for I was sent for this purpose. And He kept on preaching in the synagogues of Judea. (Luke 4:43-44).

Jesus taught the disciples not only to seek this kingdom but pray for its coming. The expression 'Thy kingdom come' is actually an imperative (3rd person aorist imperative). The rendering would be 'Let Your kingdom come' or possibly 'Lord, bring in your kingdom.' The kingdom had not come in any sense, so Christ taught His disciples to pray for His coming kingdom. Note this be foremost in prayer.[18] In prayer one

---

[18] For a good rendition or expounding of this see George Peter's *Theocratic Kingdom* proposition 105, '*The Lord's Prayer is indicative of the fact that the Church is not the covenanted Messianic Kingdom.*'

should always pray for His coming kingdom for this is part of true prayer as He taught His disciples.

"Your **kingdom** come. Your will be done, on earth as it is in heaven" (Mat. 6:10).

When His kingdom comes then 'His will' will be done on earth as it is in the heavenlies. It certainly has not been done in the past anymore than at the present.

Jesus taught His disciples to seek His kingdom and His righteousness first of all. The word 'seek' has several meanings.[19] As one seeks, he is pursuing, investigating, deliberating, expecting and other related meanings.

"But **seek first His kingdom** and His righteousness; and all these things shall be added to you" (Mat. 6:33).[20]

"But **seek for His kingdom**, and these things shall be added to you". (Luke 12:31).

Christ taught mysteries concerning the kingdom.

---

[19][UBS] ζητέω seek, search or look for; try, attempt, strive for...strive for one's own interest or advantage); want, ask, ask for; demand, require, expect; consider, deliberate, examine investigate; [Friberg, Analytic Greek Lexicon] ... of man's quest for God and what can be obtained only from him *seek, search for, try to obtain* ... of what God requires or expects from man *seek, demand* ...as making inquiry or investigation *examine, question,* ... of man's effort to obtain something *pursue, endeavor to obtain, strive for* [Liddell-Scott Greek Lexicon, Abridged] *to enquire for, ... to ask about ... to search* or *inquire into, investigate,*

[20] ζητεῖτε δὲ πρῶτον τὴν βασιλείαν [τοῦ θεοῦ] καὶ τὴν δικαιοσύνην αὐτοῦ, καὶ ταῦτα πάντα προστεθήσεται ὑμῖν (Mat. 6:33); πλὴν ζητεῖτε τὴν βασιλείαν αὐτοῦ, καὶ ταῦτα προστεθήσεται ὑμῖν (Luke 12:31), Both verses have a present active imperative which is very significant. One is to be continually seeking in the sense of investigating and expecting His coming kingdom. This is why one is to be praying for His coming and His coming kingdom. As there is no covenanted kingdom at this time, one is to seek and pray for its coming. His kingdom will be that of His righteousness reigning supreme. The church falls very short of this. Just read His take of the 7 churches of Asia in Revelation. One might even look at church history which presents a very sad and checkered past and present. If the church believes it is some form of the kingdom or kingdom now, why really pray for His coming and His coming kingdom permeated with righteousness.

"And He answered and said to them, to you it has been granted to know **the mysteries of the kingdom of heaven**, but to them it has not been granted" (Mat. 13:11).

"And He said, to you it has been granted to know **the mysteries of the kingdom of God**, but to the rest *it is* in parables, in order that seeing they may not see, and hearing they may not understand" (Luke 8:10).

His disciples (the 12) preached one kingdom

"These **twelve** Jesus sent out after instructing them, saying, Do not go in *the* way of *the* Gentiles, and do not enter *any* city of the Samaritans; but rather go to the lost sheep of the house of Israel. And as you go, preach, saying, **the kingdom of heaven** is at hand" (Mat. 10:5-7).

"And He called the **twelve** together, and gave them power and authority over all the demons, and to heal diseases. And He sent them out to proclaim **the kingdom of God**, and to perform healing" (Luke 9:1-2).

"And it came about soon afterwards, that He *began* going about from one city and village to another, proclaiming and preaching **the kingdom of God**; and the twelve were with Him" (Luke 8:1).

His kingdom was at hand

John the Baptist and Jesus actually preached the identical message.[21] They were both preaching one kingdom for

---

[21] "Now in those days John the Baptist came, preaching in the wilderness of Judea, saying, repent, for the kingdom of heaven is at hand" (Mat 3:1-2). Ἐν δὲ ταῖς ἡμέραις ἐκείναις παραγίνεται Ἰωάννης ὁ βαπτιστὴς κηρύσσων ἐν τῇ ἐρήμῳ τῆς Ἰουδαίας [καὶ] λέγων· μετανοεῖτε· <u>ἤγγικεν γὰρ ἡ βασιλεία τῶν οὐρανῶν</u>. "From that time Jesus began to preach and say, repent, for the kingdom of heaven is at hand" (Mat. 4:17). Ἀπὸ τότε ἤρξατο ὁ Ἰησοῦς κηρύσσειν καὶ λέγειν· <u>μετανοεῖτε· ἤγγικεν γὰρ ἡ βασιλεία τῶν οὐρανῶν</u>. **"For the kingdom of heaven is at hand** (ἤγγικεν γαρ ἡ Βασιλεια των οὐρανων [*ēggiken gar hē Basileia tōn ouranōn*]). Note the position of the verb and the present perfect tense. It was a startling word that John

there is only one kingdom and one King and one throne they were concerned with and no other. Scriptures teach there is only one covenanted kingdom. This is the kingdom all students of the Text should fully comprehend. All other kingdoms and thrones are of rather trivial pursuit.

"Now in those days **John the Baptist** came, preaching in the wilderness of Judea, saying, **repent, for the kingdom of heaven is at hand**" (Mat. 3:1-2).

"From that time **Jesus** began to preach and say, **repent, for the kingdom of heaven is at hand**" (Mat. 4:17).

The verb 'is at hand' ἤγγικεν is a perfect indicative in both verses. In fact the Greek is identical for the whole expression 'for the kingdom of heaven is at hand.'[22] This is significant but does not mean the kingdom has come in any sense anymore with John than it did with Jesus. The kingdom will only come and start during the day of the Lord and only after the wrath of God. Any concept of a kingdom at hand, or present, or is near, etc. in the sense of already happening or started has no biblical basis whatever. The kingdom was being preached as at hand or near. Very shortly the kingdom will not be near at all. The kingdom offer will be taken away from Israel and Israel will be left desolate for a season. Yet Israel will never be abandoned or forsaken because of the eternal covenants. In addition, the kingdom will come only after a time of His great wrath and during the day of the Lord. Much of this

---

thundered over the hills and it re-echoed throughout the land. The Old Testament prophets had said that it would come some day in God's own time. John proclaims as the herald of the new day that it has come, has drawn near. How near he does not say, but he evidently means very near, so near that one could see the signs and the proof." A.T. Robertson, *Word Pictures in the New Testament* (Nashville, TN: Broadman Press, 1933), Mt 3:2.

[22] Ἀπὸ τότε ἤρξατο ὁ Ἰησοῦς κηρύσσειν καὶ λέγειν· **μετανοεῖτε· ἤγγικεν γὰρ ἡ βασιλεία τῶν οὐρανῶν** (Mat. 4:17) Ἐν δὲ ταῖς ἡμέραις ἐκείναις παραγίνεται Ἰωάννης ὁ βαπτιστὴς κηρύσσων ἐν τῇ ἐρήμῳ τῆς Ἰουδαίας [καὶ] λέγων· **μετανοεῖτε· ἤγγικεν γὰρ ἡ βασιλεία τῶν οὐρανῶν** (Mat. 3:1-2). Note both expressions of what was being said is identical with both John and Jesus.

has already been presented in the section on the day of the Lord. All Scripture is perfectly consistent with this truth.

The covenanted lineage of the King

Mathew's gospel begins by referring first to Jesus as the son of David, "The book of the genealogy of Jesus Christ, the son of David, the son of Abraham" (Mat. 1:1). By putting David first for emphasis, Matthew is proving Jesus is not coming into the sheepfold by any other way than by the correct Davidic genealogy to assume the throne of David (Mat. 1:1-17; note vs 6). This right is given by covenanted design and decree to David's seed through Joseph, who was an heir through Solomon, David's son. Mary was in the line of David but not Solomon. He could only inherit the covenanted throne through Joseph as he is in the correct covenanted lineage.

Jesus, Israel's Messiah, is the promised and covenanted Heir Apparent to the Davidic throne as the King of Israel (Mat. 1:6). He is the King of the Jews by covenant design.[23] Matthew was not confused about the Messiah, the kingly lineage, the kingdom, the throne, and neither were certain Pharisees (John 3:1-2). Matthew was proving that this Jesus is truly God's Messiah, the One to rule over Israel, literally King of the Jews.

---

[23] Jesus will be given one throne over one kingdom as Messiah from which to reign (Dan. 7:13-14), and His kingdom will be over the Jews, the nation Israel. This kingdom will include other nations, but it will be a Jewish kingdom. The Scriptures are very clear about this covenanted kingdom. There is absolutely no doubt about this, and it is just a matter of time. It is the restored Jewish kingdom and throne and everything is heading in that direction. This is the truth of the Scriptures. Nothing less than His kingdom over the Jews will fulfill any Davidic throne or Davidic kingdom rule as Scripture reveals (Jer 23:5-8). Anything more than this or less than this simply is not covenanted. He must sit on David's throne over the Jews, the Jewish nation Israel and for this He died. "Now Jesus stood before the governor, and the governor questioned Him, saying, Are You the King of the Jews? And Jesus said to him, It is as you say" (Mat. 27:11). "And they put up above His head **the charge** against Him which read, "THIS IS **JESUS THE KING OF THE JEWS**" (Matthew 27:37).

Israel's Messiah had to be in direct lineage as the literal son of David to assume rightfully the throne and kingdom of David. However, not every son of David in the royal seed line· was qualified to rule as the king of Israel[24] (Mat. 1:12; Jer. 22:28-30). There is only one throne and kingdom of David, for the biblical covenants, especially the Davidic covenant describe but one. David knew no other, Solomon knew no other, Israel knew no other, Matthew knew no other and Jesus knew no other. For His lineage proves He is in the correct seed line, and He is the only One who has the covenanted right to the throne of David. And He is the only One Who can fulfill the Davidic covenant and quite literally all the covenants. Israel should

---

[24] "And after the deportation to Babylon, to **Jeconiah** was born Shealtiel; and to Shealtiel, Zerubbabel" (Matthew 1:12). "Is this man **Coniah** a despised, shattered jar? Or is he an undesirable vessel? Why have he and his descendants been hurled out And cast into a land that they had not known? "O land, land, land, Hear the word of the Lord! "Thus says the Lord, 'Write this man down childless, A man who will not prosper in his days; **For no man of his descendants will prosper Sitting on the throne of David Or ruling again in Judah**" (Jeremiah 22:28-30). Joseph was still a natural heir of the throne, but could not inherit the throne as such because he is in the line of Jeconiah. The rulership would pass through him as it did through the sons of Jeconiah. Had Jesus been born naturally to Joseph, He would have been disqualified from being a direct heir to the throne. But, Jesus being an adopted son, not a natural son of Joseph, the throne can still pass to Joseph's heir. "Matthew gave Jesus' lineage through His legal father, **Joseph** (v. 16). Thus this genealogy traced Jesus' right to the throne of **David,** which must come through **Solomon** and his descendants (v. 6). Of particular interest is the inclusion of **Jeconiah** (v. 11) of whom Jeremiah said, "Record this man as if childless" (Jer. 22:30). Jeremiah's prophecy related to the actual occupation of the throne and the reception of blessing while on the throne. Though Jeconiah's sons never occupied the throne, the line of rulership did pass through them. If Jesus had been a physical descendant of Jeconiah, He would not have been able to occupy David's throne. Luke's genealogy made it clear that Jesus was a physical descendant of David through another son named Nathan (Luke 3:31). But Joseph, a descendant of Solomon, was Jesus' legal father, so Jesus' right to the throne was traced through Joseph." Louis A. Barbieri, Jr., "Matthew," in *The Bible knowledge commentary, New Testament,* ed. John F. Walvoord and Roy B. Zuck (Wheaton, Ill.: Victor, 1983), 18.

have realized the time of their visitation[25] but they did not. Their rejection of Him and His offer of the kingdom will cause the removal of any kingdom being presented to them again until they say 'blessed is He Who comes in the name of the Lord.'[26]

The Pharisees and Sadducees could have challenged Jesus' right to the Davidic throne on this exact issue of His being in the correct lineage as the promised Heir and Messiah i.e. David's son to rule from David's throne. But there is not one inference, nor one word of His not being of the correct lineage of the seed of David. In fact, the genealogies given by both by Matthew (Mat. 1:1-17) and Luke (Luke 3:23-38) only accentuate His genealogy being correct, proving He is the seed of David and the only legitimate Davidic Heir to the throne and kingdom. This in itself is extremely significant and demonstrates the importance of the Davidic covenant, and its final and future fulfillment by His assumption of the throne of the kingdom of David *forever*.

He must assume this identical throne of His father David for the complete fulfillment of the Davidic covenant and all prophecy related to it. That is why some other throne such as a Davidic throne in heaven certainly violates biblical truth and is totally irrelevant. There have been no changes that have been made to the covenants, for that would not be possible because

---

[25] By Christ's very own words concerning Israel, judgment is coming instead of His covenanted kingdom blessings. "And when He approached, He saw the city and wept over it, saying, if you had known in this day, even you, the things which make for peace! But now they have been hidden from your eyes. For the days shall come upon you when your enemies will throw up a bank before you, and surround you, and hem you in on every side, and will level you to the ground and your children within you, and they will not leave in you one stone upon another, because **you did not recognize the time of your visitation**" (Luke 19:41-44).

[26] "For I say to you, from now on you shall not see Me until you say, 'Blessed is He who comes in the name of the Lord!'" (Mat. 23:39); "Behold, your house is left to you *desolate*; and I say to you, you shall not see Me until *the time* comes when you say, 'Blessed is He who comes in the name of the Lord!'"(Luke 13:35).

of their unconditional, unilateral, and eternal nature. There were neither changes nor fulfillments to the prophecies concerning the throne which arose from the covenants either (Luke 1:32-33). Christ has not ascended to the throne of David as defined by the Davidic covenant. David knew of no throne in heaven that was promised or covenanted to him in any sense. The Messiah must descend from the literal seed of David to assume the literal throne of David over literal Israel in literal Jerusalem. (Mat. 1:1-17). Anything less than this violates all of God's eternal covenants.

Israel and its leaders knew extremely well all about this, for the king of Israel must be of David's literal lineage. "The doctrine of the kingdom is first taught by covenant, theocratic ordering, and prophecy in the Old Testament, and it is taken for granted in the New Testament as a subject derived from the Old Testament and *well understood*; for the kingdom is preached without any appended explanation."[27]   Anything less than a full understanding and belief of Jesus being the Messiah and rightful Heir to David's throne from the covenanted progeny of David's seed, proves willful ignorance. All Scripture is perfectly clear on this and there is no exception or variations. There were those who were accusing Him of being illegitimate (John 8:41).[28]   However, there was never one challenge of Jesus' right to the Davidic throne and kingdom as the Messiah because He did not come in the proper Davidic lineage to assume the Davidic throne. This is most significant as this would have been one of His enemies' greatest challenges for disqualifying Him as the proper seed to take the throne of David.

This is why the people of the nation Israel were saying, questioning, and continually proclaiming things related to Jesus

---

[27] Peters, *The Theocratic Kingdom*, 1:157.

[28] "You are doing the deeds of your father." They said to Him, "We were not born in **fornication**; we have one Father, even God" (John 8:41). ὑμεῖς ποιεῖτε τὰ ἔργα τοῦ πατρὸς ὑμῶν. εἶπαν [οὖν] αὐτῷ· ἡμεῖς **ἐκ πορνείας** οὐ γεγεννήμεθα, ἕνα πατέρα ἔχομεν τὸν θεόν" "They may have been casting aspersions on Jesus birth." Edwin A Blum, "John," *The Bible knowledge commentary, New Testament*, 305.

especially in reference as coming in the covenanted line of David. The following are just a few verses concerning this exact issue, but they simply do not exhaust all the New Testament references to Jesus as the Son of David (over 50 such verses) based on the Davidic covenant concerning David's seed (2 Sam. 7:12-13). Great care should be observed in all references to Jesus being David's legal son, as He is the rightful Heir to the throne and kingdom and verified as such even by miracles (Mat. 11:2-5; 12:22-37; [29] John 3:1-2; 20:30-31).

> 1   "And all the multitudes were amazed, and began to say, This man cannot be the **Son of David**, can he?" (Matthew 12:23).

---

[29] The miracle of Mat. 12:22-37, is very significant for the Pharisees had to give an explanation to the people for this miracle. Their explanation was that Jesus certain did this but by the power of Satan. "But when the Pharisees heard it, they said, "This man casts out ἐκβάλλει τὰ δαιμόνια demons only by Beelzebul the ruler of the demons" (Matthew 12:24). They were using the present indicative signifying continuous action. The expression that Jesus used was also in the present active indicative displaying a continuous action indicating He was doing this more than this one time. "And if I by Beelzebul cast out καὶ εἰ ἐγὼ ἐν Βεελζεβοὺλ ἐκβάλλω demons, by whom do your sons cast them out? Consequently they shall be your judges" (12:27). "εἰ δὲ ἐν πνεύματι θεοῦ ἐγὼ ἐκβάλλω τὰ δαιμόνια, ἄρα ἔφθασεν ἐφ' ὑμᾶς ἡ βασιλεία τοῦ θεοῦ" (Matthew 12:28). "But if I cast out ἐκβάλλω (denotes continuous action and with the indicative and εἰ signifying a first class conditional statement, assumed as true) demons by the Spirit of God, then the kingdom of God has come upon you" (Matthew 12:28). Jesus made it very clear to them that by rejecting the miracle was one thing, but to say that it was done by the power of the enemy or Satan was quite another (12:31-32). The expression ἄρα ἔφθασεν ἐφ' ὑμᾶς ἡ βασιλεία τοῦ θεου does not mean the kingdom has come and Jesus was ruling from the throne of David over Israel forever as covenanted. There is no sense this could be true not only based on the covenants and prophecy derived from them, but Christ's kingdom will begin only over the regenerate (John 3:3-8) after the second coming (Mat. 23:39; 25:31). This crowd in Matthew 12 is hardly regenerate. They not only wanted His death (Mat. 12:14), but they did not know Satan from the God the Holy Spirit. They did not know Satan from God quite literally.

2   **"Blessed is the coming kingdom of our father David;** Hosanna in the highest!" (Mark 11:10).

3   "To a virgin engaged to a man whose name was Joseph, of the **descendants of David**; and the virgin's name was Mary" (Luke 1:27).

4   "He will be great, and will be called the Son of the Most High; and the Lord God will give Him **the throne of His father David**; and **He will reign over the house of Jacob forever; and His kingdom will have no end**" (Luke 1:32-33).

5   "And he called out, saying, **Jesus, Son of David**, have mercy on me! And those who led the way were sternly telling him to be quiet; but he kept crying out all the more, **Son of David**, have mercy on me! (Luke 18:38-39).

6   "Others were saying, this is the Christ. Still others were saying, Surely the Christ is not going to come from Galilee, is He? Has not the Scripture said that **the Christ comes from the offspring of David**, and from Bethlehem, **the village where David was**?" (John 7:41-42).

There is no other covenanted earthly throne and kingdom
The Davidic covenant established an earthly seed, an earthly house, an earthly throne, an earthly kingdom, in an earthly land, over an earthly people, Israel, the Jews. There is no heavenly rule, heavenly kingdom, nothing is being transferred or has been transferred to any other people or place. There would have been no Jew living who would have associated the throne with a heavenly one. The Messiah or the Christ is defined as the son of David exclusively from the Davidic covenant as the Heir to the Davidic throne. Any other definition simply does not apply when trying to understand the covenanted seed, the covenanted king or Messiah to rule over the Messianic or Davidic kingdom over the nation Israel from Jerusalem. Any other Messianic or kingly rule than that as covenanted by God over Israel from Jerusalem rooted in the Davidic covenant, would have no

meaning to David, his seed, or to the nation Israel. The kingdom as it is promised from the covenants and consistently developed as proven through prophecy, is one over Israel, that is the Jews, from Jerusalem, in the covenanted land. Anything less than this in referring to the throne and kingdom of David over Israel in the land, would mean absolutely nothing to David, his seed (descendants), Israel, or literally any Jew. The Messiah did not come to reign over the church, for the church is not a covenanted entity, nor is it a covenanted kingdom with a king. It may be defined that way by certain theologies, but not by biblical covenants, especially the Davidic.

It is amazing how many kingdoms are defined today as already being established, such as Christ ruling in hearts, or a heavenly rule, or Christ ruling from David's throne in heaven. Some believe a heavenly throne or rule is more spiritual, this simply is not true. George Peters made this statement over 100 years ago: "The meanings usually given to this kingdom indicate that the most vague, indefinite notions exist concerning it."[30]

The Scriptures simply do not teach multiple covenanted kingdoms, and multiple forms of the kingdom with various thrones. This is simply the neglect and oversight of the covenants. This is why there can be so much confusion, for Israel and its biblical covenants are usually not the starting points of a good systematic or biblical theology. Israel and the covenants promised to this nation are the unconditional fundamental foundation for a proper understanding of all theology, especially concerning His purpose in this world. Even the dispensations will not be properly understood without this sharp distinction.

The *sine qua non*[31] of classic dispensationalism is as true today as it was when God planned His kingdom program

---

[30] Peters, *The Theocratic Kingdom*, 1:39.

[31] The distinction of Israel and God's plan and purposes for this nation are really the key for understanding the entire bible. The sine qua non is as true today as it was when God planned His entire redemptive program. This whole argument of the covenants and especially the Davidic covenant, adds

centered in and around the nation Israel from eternity. He even set the boundaries of all the nations with reference to the nation Israel.[32] This is why it can be said to the sheep on His right "Come you who are blessed of my Father, inherit the kingdom prepared[33] for you from the foundation of the world" (Mat. 25:34). God's kingdom program if understood correctly shows unity of purpose and design for all creation (Eph. 1:10). The kingdom is far more than salvific or Christological. It becomes this if the biblical covenants are not kept in first place as the

---

much more fuel to the fire as not only is the nation Israel the key for bible interpretation; it must be for *all the covenants (the Mosaic, Abrahamic, Land, Davidic and New) are with the nation Israel, the Jew. The Jew* is the key for understanding all that God has covenanted with man. All of Scripture bears this out. "The *sine qua non* (the most basic, the minimal things) of Dispensationalism or that which marks off a man as a dispensationalist is defined by Charles Ryrie in *Dispensationalism Today* as: 1. *a dispensationalist keeps Israel and the Church distinct* 2. a consistently literal interpretation (hermeneutic) 3. underlying purpose of God in the world (dispensationalist - glory of God; covenant theology - salvation)." Charles Ryrie, *Dispensationalism Today* (Chicago: Moody Press, 1965), 43-47.

[32] "When the Most High gave the nations their inheritance, When He separated the sons of man, He set the boundaries of the peoples According to the number of the sons of Israel" (Deut.32:8). "And He made from one, every nation of mankind to live on all the face of the earth, having determined *their* appointed times, and the boundaries of their habitation" (Act 17:26). "Deut. 32:7–14. The Lord's love for Israel. God set the bounds of the nations with Israel as the center of interest, 7–9. The divine name 'Most High' is the millennial title of deity, which He will assume when the Son receives the kingdom over Israel (cf. Gen 14:19) and this prophecy is fully realized. The Lord found Israel. He encircled, cared for, prospered, and blessed her, 10–14."[32] Merrill Frederick Unger, *The New Unger's Bible Handbook*, Rev. and updated ed. (Chicago: Moody Publishers, 2005), 123.

[33] "τότε ἐρεῖ ὁ βασιλεὺς τοῖς ἐκ δεξιῶν αὐτοῦ· δεῦτε οἱ εὐλογημένοι τοῦ πατρός μου, κληρονομήσατε τὴν ἡτοιμασμένην ὑμῖν βασιλείαν ἀπὸ καταβολῆς κόσμου." (Matthew 25:34). It is important to note that the expression τὴν **ἡτοιμασμένην** ὑμῖν βασιλείαν ἀπὸ καταβολῆς κόσμου has prepared in the perfect tense. This is significant for this shows it was God's design to bring in this kingdom from all eternity. This does not mean the church does not have a calling and election also, but this expression is not used of the church, but it is of the covenanted kingdom.

foundation of Messiah's kingdom. And this must be, for the most significant design and purpose God has given concerning man will ultimately be in the kingdom of His Messiah which will be given to Jesus as the Son of man (Dan. 7:13-14; Mat. 6:33) not as the Son of God. But He must be the Son of God and the Son of man (David) to be the Messiah or Christ of Israel.

Again the kingdom and throne are very well defined and are by definition exclusively inherent to the literal seed of David and the land. Any rule from heaven simply enters into mere conjecture and speculation. Chafer makes these comments:

> Here the observation may be made that David himself believed this promise was of an earthly throne, which would not be located in heaven then or ever. It would be difficult to begin, as one so inclined must do, with David's own understanding or interpretation of Jehovah's covenant with him and then, in tracing subsequent relations between Jehovah and David's line, to find a point where the literal, earthly throne promised to David becomes a spiritual throne in heaven. David was not promised a heavenly, spiritual throne, and the one who contends that David's throne is now a heavenly rule is by so much obliged to name the time and circumstances when and where so great a change has been introduced.[34]

For David to have a heavenly throne would be much less spiritual for this would mean nothing in the covenanted kingdom program of God. There is absolutely no way David would have understood any promise in this manner. To have a

---

[34] L. S. Chafer, *Systematic Theology*, 8 vols. (Dallas: Dallas Seminary, 1948), 4:323-324.

rule from heaven, or some throne from heaven, actually diminishes and vitiates the throne of David to much less than what was promised to him. This does not fit in at all with God's covenanted program for the rule promised is over the nation Israel (Is. 9:6-7; Dan. 2:44; Luke 1:33).

God promised David that He would never take the kingdom away from him as He did with Saul. "But My lovingkindness shall not depart from him, as I took it away from Saul, whom I removed from before you" (2 Sam. 7:15). If this throne or rule were shifted to heaven or changed in any manner, God would be taking the kingdom away from David, his seed, and Israel. That would mean the covenanted kingdom had changed. The throne that was promised was of this earth, earthly, but this does not make the throne and kingdom any less spiritual. But to exalt the covenanted human throne to a place, which has some equivalency to deity, presents many problems, including a violation or breach of the promises of the Davidic covenant. To do so would be to exalt humanity and an earthly rule almost to a place of a godly rule. The Messiah has several capacities from which He is able to rule from heaven, but not from a covenanted human throne in heaven supposedly based on the Davidic covenant that defines the Davidic throne over the Jews.

It is most essential to study the details of the original Davidic covenant. The house or progeny of David is very definitely defined, for this is the royal house from which only certain ones were qualified to assume the throne of David. This in itself proves the importance of the Davidic covenant. To leave this is to demean the covenant, the promises of Jehovah, and that is less spiritual. This would literally contradict God and His kingdom program. That is why there is great warning in the New Testament as to how the nation Israel, the Jews, and the covenants are handled (Rom. 11:17-21; 28-29; Eph. 2:11-12). This definitely carries over from the original covenants and promises that were made with the nation Israel (Gen. 12:3; Jer. 31:35-37; 33:19-26). It seems this should be a wakeup call to some in the church.

The Davidic covenant is inviolable

This covenant is not only eternal and unconditional, but God makes this covenant so obviously unilateral, so completely dependent on Him, He repeats Himself at least five times: "I will not break off, I will not deal falsely, I will not violate, I will not alter the words, I will not lie" (Ps. 89:33-35). The Lord certainly did not have to say any of this at all, for He will certainly keep His Word especially His covenants. This accentuates the fact that the future restoration or restored throne and kingdom of David is virtually assured. There is no possibility of this covenant being changed or violated. Everything in it depends entirely and absolutely on God's immutable character and attributes. Nothing can violate what God has promised to Abrahamic, Isaac, Israel, and especially to David and his seed, for the Davidic covenant as well as all the other biblical covenants are assured and rendered unalterable, inviolable, and irrevocable.[35]

---

[35] (Rom. 11:28-32) "From the standpoint of the gospel they are enemies for your sake, but from the standpoint of God's choice" -note there is τὴν articulation for emphasis noting God's choice κατὰ δὲ τὴν ἐκλογὴν; **ἐκλογή, ῆς, ἡ**— selection, election as t.t. (technical term) for choosing: Walter Bauer, A Greek-English Lexicon of the New Testament and other Early Christian Literature, 2nd ed., rev. F. Wilbur Gingrich and Frederick W. Danker, trans. (Chicago: University of Chicago Press, 1957, 1979), 243. **They (the Jews, Israel, His chosen nation) κατὰ δὲ τὴν ἐκλογὴν** (lit. according to the election) **are beloved for the sake of the fathers**; for the gifts and the calling of God are irrevocable ἀμεταμέλητα (11:29). "For just as you once were disobedient to God, but now have been shown mercy because of their disobedience, so these also now have been disobedient, in order that because of the mercy shown to you they also may now be shown mercy. For God has shut up all in disobedience that He might show mercy to all" (Romans 11:30-32). Paul is discussing the irrevocable calling of the nation Israel. The fullness of the Gentiles will come in (11:25) and that is most likely when the last Gentile believes that Jesus is the Christ. Then God will deal immediately with His chosen nation Israel because of the fathers and the gifts (lovingkindness, mercy, most of all the covenants) displayed to Israel's fathers, for the gifts and the calling of God are irrevocable. "ἀμεταμέλητα γὰρ τὰ χαρίσματα καὶ ἡ κλῆσις τοῦ θεοῦ" (Romans 11:29). Note that ἀμεταμέλητα is first for emphasis. Paul is stressing the future of

Therefore, no exegesis, no theology, no reading back into these biblical covenants from the New Testament, no altering of any words, no altering of any promises, nothing based on later revelation, no infringement of one tittle can be allowed without God becoming less than God or a liar. If God is all that He has declared Himself to be, then He will carry out the Davidic covenant literally, for He will never lie.

"I will not lie to David For the sake of David Thy servant, Do not turn away the face of Thine anointed. **The Lord has sworn to David, A truth from which He will not turn back; "Of the fruit of your body I will set upon your throne.** If your sons will keep My covenant, And My testimony which I will teach them, Their sons also shall sit upon your throne forever. **For the Lord has chosen Zion; He has desired it for His habitation.** This is **My resting place forever**; Here I will dwell, for I have desired it. "I will abundantly bless her provision; I will satisfy her needy with bread. "Her priests also I will clothe with salvation; And her godly ones will sing aloud for joy. **There I will cause the horn of David to spring forth**; I have prepared a lamp for **Mine anointed**. His enemies I will clothe with shame; but upon himself his crown shall shine" (Psalm 132:10-18).

Israel is based on the very initial calling of the fathers (patriarchs) and that there is absolutely nothing that can change or violate the course of progression in God's program until a complete fulfillment is attained in the completed redemption of the nation Israel. "and thus all Israel will be saved; just as it is written, "The Deliverer will come from Zion, He will remove ungodliness from Jacob." (Romans 11:26) ἀμεταμέλητος, ον—1. not to be regretted, without regret .... μετάνοια repentance not to be regretted ... Hence also irrevocable, of something one does not take back ... 2. feeling no remorse, having no regret; Walter Bauer, *A Greek-English Lexicon of the New Testament and other Early Christian Literature*, 45.

This Psalm also shows the greatness and significance of the Davidic covenant. Psalm 132 makes it extremely clear that God will keep the promises to David, and He swears not to turn back from keeping the truth. "The Lord has sworn to David, a truth from which He will not turn back." There is really no need for repetition, but in case there are some who are not taking what God has promised to David, to Israel, *the Jews*, contained in the covenants very seriously, and holding on to them tenaciously as the basis for a complete biblical theology (Rom. 11:29), God repeats Himself many times. This does not take very much to comprehend and understand. God is totally committed to completing His kingdom program, that which He has spelled out concerning the throne with David in the Davidic covenant. It is virtually impossible not to have an understanding of all this unless one's system of theology and understanding the Scripture does not permit it. Again, God is serious about all this for His Holiness is literally on the line (Ps. 89:35).

The throne and kingdom were unconditional
"For the sake of David Thy servant, do not turn away the face of Thine anointed. The Lord has sworn to David, A truth from which He will not turn back; "Of the fruit of your body I will set upon your throne. If your sons will keep My covenant, And My testimony which I will teach them, Their sons also shall sit upon your throne forever" (Ps. 132:10-11). What is interesting about this Psalm especially here is that the Psalmist is speaking of a literal descendant of David who must reign from David's throne, *"of the fruit of your body I will set upon your throne."* This has to be understood exclusively as a rule from David's covenanted throne over the covenanted kingdom (2 Sam. 7:16). This is the literal throne of David over the literal kingdom of Israel (1 Chron. 28:5; 29:32; 2 Chron. 7:18; 9:8). David could have not understood this throne to be anything else, for there is no other covenant related to the throne of David that is a covenant which changes any promise of the covenant itself.

The promise here is that David's sons would remain perpetually on David's throne if they were obedient. They were not obedient, but this does not annul or change any of the promises of the covenant. The promises of the covenant anticipate the discipline that will come on the house of David (2 Sam. 7:14-15; 1 Kings 9:4-9; 11:9-13), Solomon (1 Kings 11:9-13), and David himself (2 Sam. 12:7-14). Nevertheless, this does not invalidate any of the promises in any way, which is simply not possible.

All of this refers to a literal throne and kingdom over a literal people in the literal land. Even the land promise as the basis of the Abrahamic covenant, which is consistent throughout the covenants, has to be literal Zion. "For the Lord has chosen Zion; He has desired it for His habitation" (Ps. 132:13).   The Psalmist is not referring to some heavenly sphere or location, or the third heaven itself. He is speaking of literal Zion, from which the seed of David must reign from the literal covenanted throne in Jerusalem.

Everything in this world is progressing toward this covenanted kingdom. This proves also a unity of design and purpose to the creation (Mat. 6:10, 33; 25:34; Acts 1:6; 28:31; 2 Tim 4:1). For anything, less than this is simply not the biblically restored kingdom and throne of David. The throne and kingdom of David must be the covenanted Jewish throne and kingdom as promised to David in the covenant. It must be centered in Jerusalem, and it cannot be given to another people or race. Anything violating the rule of David from David's throne in Jerusalem violates every promise in the Davidic covenant. This also would abrogate the covenant itself and the other biblical covenants, and would simply present a bogus rule or kingdom and one much less spiritual because of all the violated promises. John Walvoord comments:

> The meaning of the Davidic Covenant, as explained in Scripture in 2 Samuel 7 and 1 Chronicles 17 and amplified by Psalm 89, is relatively easy to understand. God entered into

solemn covenant with David, promising that
both his throne and his lineage would continue
forever. Because such an expectation was
contrary to ordinary history, David himself
raised the question in 2 Samuel 7:18-19 about
the unusual longevity to the promise. But it is
clear that David understood the promise to
extend to his political rule over Israel and to
succession on the throne of those descended
from David. Such an interpretation seems
natural to the scriptural record of the Davidic
Covenant.[36]

Even unto David's last breath, he understood what had
been promised to him, and it was very much still contained in
an eternal covenant. "For He has made an everlasting covenant
with me" (2 Sam. 23:5).

"Now these are the last words of David. David
the son of Jesse declares, And the man who was
raised on high declares, The anointed of the God
of Jacob, And the sweet psalmist of Israel, The
Spirit of the Lord spoke by me, And His word
was on my tongue. The God of Israel said, The
Rock of Israel spoke to me, 'He who rules over
men righteously, Who rules in the fear of God, Is
as the light of the morning when the sun rises, A
morning without clouds, When the tender grass
springs out of the earth, Through sunshine after
rain.' **Truly is not my house so with God? For
He has made an everlasting covenant with me,
Ordered in all things, and secured; for all my
salvation and all my desire, Will He not
indeed make it grow?** But the worthless, every

---

[36] John F. Walvoord, *The Prophecy Knowledge Handbook*, (Wheaton: Victor
Books, 1990), 57.

one of them will be thrust away like thorns, because they cannot be taken in hand; but the man who touches them must be armed with iron and the shaft of a spear, and they will be completely burned with fire in their place." (2 Samuel 23:1-7).

Jesus is the covenanted King of the Jews.

Only the true son of David in the true kingly line may claim the covenanted and authorized throne of David as King of the Jews. For this He truly died. Again, was Jesus the correct one or not? The biblical covenants and specifically the Davidic covenant define this kingly line (Mat. 1:1-17). Is the kingdom to be restored to the Jews or not?

- "And they put up above His head the charge against Him which read, "THIS IS JESUS THE KING OF THE JEWS" (Matthew 27:37).
- "And the inscription of the charge against Him read, "THE KING OF THE JEWS" (Mark 15:26).
- "Now there was also an inscription above Him, "THIS IS THE KING OF THE JEWS" (Luke 23:38).
- "And Pilate wrote an inscription also, and put it on the cross. And it was written, "JESUS THE NAZARENE, THE KING OF THE JEWS" (John 19:19).

Conclusion

God has planned and covenanted a kingdom. He is going to carry out His sovereign will with His creation. God has graciously told man exactly what He wants him to know concerning what He is going to do with His people and His Anointed. Only a loving Sovereign would tell His creatures what He is going to do. He has spelled this out in detail with His eternal, unconditional, unilateral covenants.

> The greater the work contemplated – and there is none great than this kingdom – the more clearly ought we to see the intelligence of the Mind that originates it, and the power of the Will that performs it. If that Mind and Will has proposed, in Revelation to man, a certain, determinate plan of operation by which the kingdom shall, after a while, be openly revealed; if the design and mode of procedure and result commends itself to faith and reason as adapted and desirable; if history and experience plainly sustains the developments of such a plan through the ages, *then* we may rest assured that in harmony with such a purposed plan, with its corroborating history and adjustment to the necessities of man and creation, there must be, as the Bible wisely and scientifically affirms, a guiding mind and controlling will.[37]

---

[37] Peters, *The Theocratic Kingdom,* 1:37-38.

Chapter 9
The Kingdom of Israel was Removed

Discipline was promised as covenanted

As it has been biblically shown the kingdom was covenanted exclusively with David and his seed and absolutely no one else. In the original Davidic covenant, David and his seed were promised an eternal throne and kingdom which would never be taken away. It must be continually remembered that there is only one kingdom and one throne covenanted with David and his son.

Note the throne and kingdom are *forever*.

1. When your days are complete and you lie down with your fathers (*David*)

2. **I will raise up your descendant after you**, who will come forth from you, and **I will establish his kingdom.** He (*David's son*) shall build a house for My name, and

3. **I will establish the throne of his kingdom _forever_** (*David's son*)

4. I will be a father to him and he will be a son to Me; when he commits iniquity, I will correct him with the rod of men and the strokes of the sons of men, but My lovingkindness shall not depart from him (*David's son*), as I took *it* away from Saul, whom I removed from before you.

5. **And your house and your kingdom shall endure before Me _forever_, your throne shall be established _forever_** (*David*) (2 Sam.7:12-16).

There was also promised discipline concerning David's son when David's son was ruling from the covenanted throne and kingdom in Jerusalem. "I will be a father to him and he will be a son to Me; when he commits iniquity, I will correct him with the rod of men and the strokes of the sons of men, but My lovingkindness shall not depart from him, as I took *it* away from Saul, whom I removed from before you" (2 Sam. 7:14).

This was God's proving Himself a Father to His reigning king of the covenanted kingdom. God treated the anointed of His kingdom as a son. This was a true relationship of a Father and son and His discipline was very real.

The Lord is Sovereign and He declares as such concerning His covenanted king/s and kingdom, yet God's discipline always displays His mercy, love, and grace. David certainly understood this very well. Even as the reigning king of Israel, David was thoroughly disciplined by the One Who established him, his kingdom, his kingly reign, and his seed. David also understood the Lord's grace and forgiveness.

> "How blessed is he whose transgression is forgiven, whose sin is covered! How blessed is the man to whom the LORD does not impute iniquity, and in whose spirit there is no deceit! When I kept silent *about my sin*, my body wasted away through my groaning all day long. For day and night Thy hand was heavy upon me; my vitality was drained away *as* with the fever heat of summer. Selah. I acknowledged my sin to Thee, and my iniquity I did not hide; I said, I will confess my transgressions to the LORD; And Thou didst forgive the guilt of my sin" (Ps. 32:1-5).

God promised Fatherly discipline to David and his ruling progeny of kings, but He also promised that the throne and kingdom of David and his seed were forever or eternal. As God may discipline His kings as sons over Israel, He will never abrogate the covenanted throne and kingdom promised to David and his seed. The Davidic seed and throne were forever.

- "I have made a covenant with My chosen; I have sworn to David My servant, <u>I will establish your seed forever, And build up your throne to all generations</u>" (Ps. 89:3-4).

- "I have found David My servant; <u>With My holy oil I have anointed him, with whom My hand will be established</u>; My arm also will strengthen him" (Ps. 89:20-21).

- "My lovingkindness I will keep for him forever, and My covenant shall be confirmed to him. <u>So I will establish his *descendants* forever, and his throne as the days of heaven</u>" (Ps. 89:28-29).

Even though the above is all part of the Davidic covenant especially that of David's progeny in the royal seed line, discipline was also a vital and promised part of the covenant. This is even enhanced in the Psalms. "If <u>his sons</u> forsake My law, And do not walk in My judgments, if they violate My statutes, And do not keep My commandments, then I will visit their transgression with the rod, And their iniquity with stripes" (Ps. 89:30-32).

The Lord may even remove the covenanted king as He chooses as a disciplinary measure to protect the throne and the kingdom. The Lord did take away the throne and kingdom from Saul, this is true. However, there was never a covenanted kingdom and throne with Saul in any manner.

Even though He took the kingdom from Saul, He will never take away the promised eternal throne and kingdom from David and his seed. For not only is the covenant eternal so is the covenanted throne and kingdom. If He did remove the throne and kingdom from David and/or his seed, this would not only violate His eternal covenants He has made with an oath,[1] but it would violate Who God is by His very nature and Word. He effectively placed His Word above His name. "I will worship toward Your holy temple, and praise Your name For Your lovingkindness and Your truth; for <u>You have magnified Your word above all Your name</u>" (Ps. 138:2 NKJ).[2] One is not only known by his word, you are your word. This God has established, for His Word is forever and cannot err for His is the Lord and cannot change.[3] "Forever, O LORD, Thy word is settled in heaven" (Ps. 119:89).

The kingdom removed

God had warned Israel through His prophets by sending many prophets continually warning them to turn from their evil ways. The northern kingdom had been taken captive first about 722 B.C. by Assyria[4] because of their evil and adulterous ways.

---

[1] "I have made a covenant with My chosen; I have sworn to David My servant, I will establish your seed forever, And build up your throne to all generations" (Ps. 89:3-4); "Once I have sworn by My holiness; I will not lie to David. His descendants shall endure forever, and his throne as the sun before Me. It shall be established forever like the moon, and the witness in the sky is faithful" (Ps. 89:35-37).

[2] "I will bow down toward Thy holy temple, And give thanks to Thy name for Thy lovingkindness and Thy truth; For Thou hast magnified Thy word <u>according to all Thy name</u>" (Ps. 138:2NASB). This is the usual rendering in most translations. But note the preposition before 'all Thy (Your) name' עַל which usually means on, upon, over, on account of (Langerscheidt). Yet the New King James renders this truly to form :"I will worship toward Your holy temple, And praise Your name For Your lovingkindness and Your truth; For You have magnified Your word **above** all Your name'(NKJ). You are as good as your word and you are known by your word.

[3] "For I, the LORD, do not change; therefore you, O sons of Jacob, are not consumed" (Mal 3:6). "For His lovingkindness is great toward us, And the truth of the LORD is everlasting. Praise the LORD!" (Ps. 117:2).

[4] Hoshea was the last king of Israel that is the northern kingdom (732–722 B.C.), "Hoshea was dominated and heavily taxed by Assyria. He was imprisoned for conspiracy with Egypt, his capital Samaria was besieged, and its citizens carried captive 722 B.C. The 200-year old northern kingdom collapsed, the result of its incurable apostasies, 7–23." Merrill Frederick

This captivity and exile was also a warning to the southern kingdom for them to take heed as to their drifting from Him. If the covenanted nations had listened to His warnings, He would have graciously let them stay in their covenanted land and kingdom. But this was not to be. The northern and southern kingdoms did not listen to any of His warnings. They totally forsook Him, His prophets, and His many appeals to turn back to Him.

They continued in their idolatrous ways therefore bringing His judgments on themselves. "Because the people had repeatedly rejected God's warnings, God would summon the Babylonians (the peoples of the north). ...Their leader, Nebuchadnezzar, was called God's servant in the sense that he would do God's bidding in coming to destroy Jerusalem. God would use the Babylonians to completely destroy both Judah and her allies. The sounds of joy and gladness would cease (cf. Jer. 7:34; 16:9) in the nation because the whole country would become a desolate wasteland when Babylon was finished. God would deport Judah and the other rebellious people to Babylon to serve the Babylonians 70 years."[5]

> "Therefore thus says the LORD of hosts,
> 'Because you have not obeyed My words,
> behold, I will send and take all the families of the
> north, declares the LORD, 'and *I will send* to
> Nebuchadnezzar king of Babylon, My servant,
> and will bring them against this land, and against
> its inhabitants, and against all these nations
> round about; and I will utterly destroy them, and
> make them a horror, and a hissing, and an
> everlasting desolation. Moreover, I will take
> from them the voice of joy and the voice of

Unger, *The New Unger's Bible Handbook*, Rev. and updated ed. (Chicago: Moody Publishers, 2005), 192-93.
[5] Charles H. Dyer, "Jeremiah" In , in *The Bible Knowledge Commentary: An Exposition of the Scriptures*, ed. J. F. Walvoord and R. B. Zuck (Wheaton, IL: Victor Books, 1985), Je 25:1–26.

gladness, the voice of the bridegroom and the
voice of the bride, the sound of the millstones
and the light of the lamp. And this whole land
shall be a desolation and a horror, and these
nations shall serve the king of Babylon seventy
years" (Jer. 25:8-11).

What is most interesting is God choosing a gentile king
such as Nebuchadnezzar the king of Babylon to do His bidding.
As Israel embraced idolatry, He gave them into the idolatrous
nation of Babylon for 70 years.[6] Note well this prophecy in
Jeremiah concerning Nebuchadnezzar king of Babylon (Jer.
27:5-8).

"I have made the earth, the men and the beasts
which are on the face of the earth by My great
power and by My outstretched arm, and I will
give it to the one who is pleasing in My sight.
And now I have given all these lands into the
hand of Nebuchadnezzar king of Babylon, My
servant, and I have given him also the wild
animals of the field to serve him. And all the

---

[6]"And this whole land shall be a desolation and a horror, and these nations
shall serve the king of Babylon seventy years" (Jer. 25:11). "Why did God
predict that the Babylonian Exile would last 70 years? (605-536 B.C.) The
answer seems to be that this was the number of years that the people had
failed to observe God's Law of a "Sabbath rest" for the land. God had
decreed that every seventh year the land was to lie fallow (Lev. 25:3–5). The
people were not to sow their fields or prune their vineyards. If the people
would fail to follow this command, God would remove them from the land
to enforce this "Sabbath rest" (Lev. 26:33–35). The writer of 2 Chronicles
indicated that the 70-year Babylonian Captivity promised by Jeremiah
allowed the land to enjoy its "Sabbath rest" (2 Chron. 36:20–21). Therefore
the Captivity lasted 70 years probably because this was the number of
Sabbath rests that had not been observed for the land." Charles H. Dyer,
"Jeremiah" In , in *The Bible Knowledge Commentary: An Exposition of the
Scriptures*, ed. J. F. Walvoord and R. B. Zuck (Wheaton, IL: Victor Books,
1985), Je 25:8–11.

nations shall serve him, and his son, and his grandson, until the time of his own land comes; then many nations and great kings will make him their servant. And it will be, *that* the nation or the kingdom which will not serve him, Nebuchadnezzar king of Babylon, and which will not put its neck under the yoke of the king of Babylon, I will punish that nation with the sword, with famine, and with pestilence, declares the LORD, until I have destroyed it by his hand" (Jer. 27:5-8).

This begins what is known as the times of the Gentiles. This can be defined when there is no monarch ruling from David's throne. The throne or rule of David had been removed from Israel as there was no ruling king on David's throne over David's kingdom. Remember there was promised discipline to David's sons who sat over the throne and kingdom of Israel. Many of the kings were drawn to idolatry and did nothing about it but embrace it. This does not mean the throne or the kingdom had been removed forever, for this is not possible based on the eternal Davidic covenant.

Also, note that there is no covenant made with Nebuchadnezzar king of Babylon or the people of Babylon. This means the scepter had been removed from the Davidic throne of Israel. It will be removed until the nail pierced hands of the Lord Jesus takes it back. Only then will the throne and kingdom of Israel be restored. This is exactly why His disciples asked Him "And so when they had come together, they were asking Him, saying, Lord, is it at this time You are restoring[7]

---

[7] "And so when they had come together, they were asking Him, saying, "Lord, is it at this time You are **restoring** the kingdom to Israel?" (Acts 1:6). Οἱ μὲν οὖν συνελθόντες ἠρώτων αὐτὸν λέγοντες· κύριε, εἰ ἐν τῷ χρόνῳ τούτῳ **ἀποκαθιστάνεις** τὴν βασιλείαν τῷ Ἰσραήλ; [UBS] **ἀποκαθίστημι** and ἀποκαθιστάνω (fut. ἀποκαταστήσω ; aor. ἀπεκατέστην ; aor. pass. ἀπεκατεστάθην) reestablish, restore; cure, make well; send or bring back (He

the kingdom to Israel?" (Acts1:6). He is the only One qualified to restore this covenanted kingdom. For this is His kingdom by divine right as He is the only legitimate Heir Apparent to not only restore the throne and kingdom, but to sit on this throne and rule. This will only happen at His second coming during the day of the Lord. Then He will take His covenanted Davidic throne over Israel and reign for 1,000 years (Rev. 20:1-4).

The delay of the restored kingdom

The covenanted kingdom cannot and will not be restored until 'the times of the Gentiles' come to an end or are fulfilled (Luke 21:24). This will only happen in the day of the Lord at the second coming of Christ.

The book of Daniel presents three separate visions in sequence. The first of these was given to Nebuchadnezzar king of Babylon, and the following two visions were given to Daniel. These visions identify 'the times of the Gentiles' which are the final four gentile kingdoms, before the second coming of Christ to set up His kingdom. He is the smiting stone Who destroys those kingdoms and then His kingdom will fill the whole earth (Dan. 2:34-35).

The eternal Son of God, the Lord Jesus, the Messiah, the Christ of Israel will finally ascend to the covenanted Davidic throne[8] of His kingdom. 'Thy/Your kingdom come' will then be fulfilled not only for answered prayers of His saints,[9] but to fulfill the eternal covenants.

13.19); [Friberg] ... strictly restore to an earlier condition; hence (1) restore, establish again (AC 1.6); [Liddell-Scott] to re-establish, restore, reinstate.

[8] "For a child will be born to us, a son will be given to us; And the government will rest on His shoulders; and His name will be called Wonderful Counselor, Mighty God, Eternal Father, Prince of Peace. There will be no end to the increase of *His* government or of peace, on the throne of David and over his kingdom, to establish it and to uphold it with justice and righteousness From then on and forevermore. The zeal of the LORD of hosts will accomplish this" (Is. 9:6-7).

[9] "Thy kingdom come. Thy will be done, on earth as it is in heaven" (Mat. 6:10).

Nebuchadnezzar king of Babylon

Nebuchadnezzar king of Babylon, God's chosen servant, was deeply plagued by many dreams. "Now in the second year of the reign[10] of Nebuchadnezzar, Nebuchadnezzar had dreams; and his spirit was troubled and his sleep left him. Then the king gave orders to call in the magicians, the conjurers, the sorcerers and the Chaldeans, to tell the king his dreams. So they came in and stood before the king" (Dan 2:1-2).

This was a vision of a great statue given to Nebuchadnezzar in a dream by God (Dan. 2:31-35). Daniel was the only one who could reveal the dream and the interpretation. Daniel described the vision of the statue (Dan. 2:31-35) and then gave the interpretation to the king (Dan. 2:37-41).

Nebuchadnezzar's vision

"You, O king, were looking and behold, there was a single great statue; that statue, which was large and of extraordinary splendor, was standing in front of you, and its appearance was awesome.

- The head of that statue *was made* of fine gold
- Its breast and its arms of silver,
- Its belly and its thighs of bronze
- Its legs of iron
- Its feet partly of iron and partly of clay

You continued looking until a stone was cut out without hands, and it struck the statue on its feet of iron and clay, and crushed them. Then the iron, the clay, the bronze, the silver and the gold were crushed all at the same time, and became like chaff from the summer threshing floors; and the wind carried them away so that not a trace of them was found. But the stone that struck the

---

[10] His reign began in 605 B.C. so this is possibly 603 B.C.

statue became a great mountain and filled the whole earth" (Dan 2:31-35).

<u>Daniel was given the interpretation</u>
"You, O king, are the king of kings, to whom the God of heaven has given the kingdom, the power, the strength, and the glory; and wherever the sons of men dwell, *or* the beasts of the field, or the birds of the sky, He has given *them* into your hand and has caused you to rule over them all.[11]

- <u>You are the head of gold</u>. And after you
- There will arise another <u>kingdom</u> inferior to you,
- Then another <u>third</u> <u>kingdom</u> of bronze, which will rule over all the earth.
- Then there will be a <u>fourth kingdom</u> as strong as iron; inasmuch as iron crushes and shatters all things, so, like iron that breaks in pieces, it will crush and break all these in pieces. And in that you saw the feet and toes, partly of potter's clay and partly of iron, it will be a <u>divided kingdom</u>; but <u>it will have in it the toughness of iron, inasmuch as you saw the iron mixed with common clay. And *as* the toes of the feet *were* partly of iron and partly of pottery, *so* some of the kingdom will be strong and part of it will be brittle</u>" (Dan 2:37-41)

Note that Daniel was describing four successive gentile world kingdoms. The first kingdom was Babylon and the head of gold represented Nebuchadnezzar. The following metal parts

---

[11]Note this is the kingdom promised by God to Nebuchadnezzar king of Babylon (Jer. 27:5-8).

of the statue which represented successive gentile kingdoms became more and more inferior. Not only do the metals demonstrate this, but the significance of those kingdoms becomes more and more inferior i.e. inferior in rank, status, and quality.

Note again the material or metals of the image are deteriorating in quality. This is significant to the interpretation and noted by Daniel (Dan. 2:36-43). A summary of the vision of the image and interpretation up to now would look something like this.

- Head of gold – Nebuchadnezzar king of Babylon
- Breast and arms of silver – another kingdom, inferior to Babylon
- Belly and thighs of bronze – defined the 3rd kingdom
- Legs of iron – defined as the 4th kingdom
- Feet partly of iron and clay -- final form of 4th kingdom

The Lord revealed to Daniel the image itself and the metals represented successively inferior kingdoms. This is a vision and representation of the final four gentile world kingdoms known technically as the times of the Gentiles when there is no covenanted Davidic king ruling from the Davidic throne in Jerusalem. Again, a Davidic rule in heaven was never covenanted, never given in any sense to David and his seed, and is simply nowhere to be found in the Text.[12]

Nebuchadnezzar king of Babylon was definitively defined, but the names of the other three gentile kings or

---

[12]It is quite sad and tragic how the eternal covenants give way to mere speculation and theory of a kingdom now, building His kingdom now, a Davidic throne in heaven, a kingdom of Christ ruling in the heart, a kingdom already but not yet, etc. Why ramble on the inferior and spend so much effort on that which is simply a mirage of someone's thoughts and speculations when He has given His literal Word of eternal covenants and sealed them with His Own Son's literal blood?

kingdoms were not defined in this vision and interpretation.[13] "The revelation and interpretation of the dream. By divine help in answer to prayer, Nebuchadnezzar's forgotten dream was revealed by Daniel, 31–35, and interpreted to the king, 36–45. The large statue or colossus, as interpreted by Daniel, symbolizes the entire period known in prophecy as the times of the Gentiles (Lk 21:24)... This is the long era when Jerusalem is politically subservient to the nations, among whom the chosen people are not to be reckoned (Num 23:9). It began with Judah's initial captivity to Babylon in 605 B.C., and will extend to the second advent of Messiah, the Smiting Stone, 34–35, who will destroy the Gentile world system catastrophically."[14]

Daniel's interpretation identifies the legs of iron as the 4th kingdom. There is more information given on this fourth kingdom and its final form than all of the other kingdoms combined. "Then there will be a fourth kingdom as strong as iron; inasmuch as iron crushes and shatters all things, so, like iron that breaks in pieces, it will crush and break all these in pieces" (Dan. 2:40). There are no more kingdoms such as a fifth gentile world empire. It should be observed that each successive gentile kingdom takes over or destroys the previous kingdom. Yet this fourth kingdom will crush the previous three kingdoms. Even Babylon was to be devoured or destroyed by the following gentile kingdom.[15] "Thus the Babylonian threat

---

[13]But much more detail will be given to Daniel in several visions identifying these kings and kingdoms in chapters 7 and 8 of Daniel. Daniel in his vision of the beasts in chapter 7 is almost a back to back vision of that of Nebuchadnezzar.

[14]Merrill Frederick Unger, *The New Unger's Bible Handbook*, Rev. and updated ed. (Chicago: Moody Publishers, 2005), 310.

[15]"I have made the earth, the men and the beasts which are on the face of the earth by My great power and by My outstretched arm, and I will give it to the one who is pleasing in My sight. <u>And now I have given all these lands into the hand of Nebuchadnezzar king of Babylon, My servant, and I have given him also the wild animals of the field to serve him.</u> And all the nations shall serve him, and his son, and his grandson, until the time of his own land comes; **then many nations and great kings will make him their servant.** And it will be, *that* the nation or the kingdom which will not serve him,

was not to be only temporary, as the false prophets glibly promised. When the appointed time came for the termination of Babylonian supremacy, the rulers of Persia, Media, and contiguous areas finally overthrew it. God is Creator of the universe and Administrator in the affairs of the nations."[16] In other words these gentile kingdoms were/are temporal and progressively inferior and not eternal as the covenanted kingdom of David and his son.

There was also included in the vision a stone which struck the image on the feet which were of iron and clay. Again, the feet do not present a fifth kingdom but a latter or final form from the legs of iron of the last gentile kingdom or world empire. This final form of the kingdom is identified as feet and toes. The feet with the 10 toes appear to be representing the final form of the gentile world kingdom representing 10 kings.

1. "And <u>in the days of those kings</u>
2. <u>The God of heaven will set up a kingdom which will never be destroyed,</u>
3. And *that* kingdom will not be left for another people;
4. It will crush and put an end to all these kingdoms,
5. <u>But it will itself endure forever.</u>
6. Inasmuch as you saw that a stone was cut out of the mountain without hands and that it crushed the iron, the bronze, the clay, the silver, and the gold, <u>the great God has made known to the king what will take place in the future;</u> so the dream is

---

Nebuchadnezzar king of Babylon, and which will not put its neck under the yoke of the king of Babylon, I will punish that nation with the sword, with famine, and with pestilence, declares the LORD, until I have destroyed it by his hand" (Jer. 27:5-8). The Babylonian take over was not only promised by the Lord, but it was at best temporary.

[16]Gaebelein, Frank E., General Editor, *The Expositor Bible Commentary*, (Grand Rapids: Regency Reference Library, Zondervan, 1986). 544.

true, and its interpretation is trustworthy" (Dan. 2:44-45).

This is a very significant part of the interpretation of Nebuchadnezzar's vision. In the days of the 10 kings (10 toes) or final form of the gentile world empire, God will set up a kingdom which will never be destroyed. This is also directly related to that stone that struck this image and filled the whole earth. "Then the iron, the clay, the bronze, the silver and the gold were crushed all at the same time, and became like chaff from the summer threshing floors; and the wind carried them away so that not a trace of them was found. But the stone that struck the statue became a great mountain and filled the whole earth" (Dan. 2:35). "Daniel's interpretation makes it clear that the image revealed the course of Gentile kingdoms which in turn would rule over the land of Palestine and the people of Israel. Nebuchadnezzar, head of the Babylonian Empire, was represented by the head of gold (v. 38). His father had come to power in Babylon by military conquest, but Nebuchadnezzar received his dominion and power and might and glory from God (who sets up kings and deposes them, v. 21)... Nebuchadnezzar's rule was viewed as a worldwide empire, in which he ruled over all mankind as well as over beasts and birds. At the time of Creation the right to rule over the earth was given man who was to have dominion over it and all the creatures in it (Gen. 1:26). Here Nebuchadnezzar by divine appointment was helping fulfill what God had planned for man."[17]

The times of the Gentiles and the latter days of Israel run concurrently. These will both end in the day of the Lord at the second coming of Jesus Christ. He will then put an end to the times of the Gentiles, purge Israel and all rebellion, and then He

---

[17] J. Dwight Pentecost, "Daniel" In , in *The Bible Knowledge Commentary: An Exposition of the Scriptures*, ed. J. F. Walvoord and R. B. Zuck (Wheaton, IL: Victor Books, 1985), Dan. 2:36–39.

will establish His covenanted throne and kingdom. The latter days of the church end at the rapture of the church.

Daniel's first vision of 4 beasts

Daniel had at least two separate visions which are recorded in Daniel chapters 7 and 8. As Nebuchadnezzar's vision was that of a colossal statue of gold, silver, bronze, and iron, Daniel's visions were that of various ravenous beasts effectively devouring one another.

Daniel's first vision almost parallels that of Nebuchadnezzar but was some time later. This vision was of four wild beasts representing four kings. Daniel was also given much more revelation in a subsequent vision which presents more details identifying two of these gentile kings and their world empires.

"In the first year of Belshazzar[18] king of Babylon Daniel saw a dream and visions in his mind *as he lay* on his bed; then he wrote the dream down *and* related the *following* summary of it. Daniel said, I was looking in my vision by night, and behold, the four winds of heaven were stirring up the great sea. And four great beasts were coming up from the sea, different from one another" (Dan 7:1-3).

1. The first *was* like a lion and had *the* wings of an eagle. I kept looking until its wings were plucked, and it was lifted up from the ground and made to stand on two feet like a man; a human mind also was given to it.
2. And behold, another beast, a second one, resembling a bear. And it was raised up on one side, and three ribs *were* in its mouth between its teeth; and thus they said to it, 'Arise, devour much meat!
3. After this I kept looking, and behold, another one, like a leopard, which had on its back four wings of a bird; the beast also had four heads, and dominion was given to it.

---

[18]This is usually dated about 553 B.C. approximately 14 years before the fall of Babylon.

4. After this I kept looking in the night visions, and behold, a <u>fourth beast, dreadful and terrifying and extremely strong; and it had large iron teeth</u>. It devoured and crushed, and trampled down the remainder with its feet; and it was different from all the beasts that were before it, and it had ten horns. (Dan 7:3-7).

The interpretation was revealed to Daniel. "These great beasts, which are four *in number*, are four kings *who* will arise from the earth" (7:17).

<u>Lion</u> -- king 1
<u>Bear</u> -- king 2
<u>Leopard</u> -- king 3
<u>Terrifying beast</u> -- king 4

Daniel's vision of the four beasts represented four kings. As Nebuchadnezzar's vision was primarily related to gentile kingdoms, Daniel's first vision was that of four gentile kings but this will also include their kingdoms.

Daniel wanted to know the precise meaning of the fourth beast (7:19). "Then I desired to know <u>the exact meaning of the fourth beast</u>, which was different from all the others, exceedingly dreadful, with its teeth of iron and its claws of bronze, *and which* devoured, crushed, and trampled down the remainder with its feet, <u>and *the meaning* of the ten horns that *were* on its head, and the other *horn* which came up, and before which three *of them* fell,</u> namely, that horn which had eyes and a mouth uttering great *boasts*, and which was larger in appearance than its associates" (Dan 7:19-20).

Daniel was told the meaning of the fourth beast with the 10 horns. Note that the forth beast is defined as a forth kingdom on the earth. Daniel understood all this as *literal*. The bible student can learn much by Daniel's method of interpreting prophecy.

1. "The fourth beast will be a fourth kingdom on the earth, which will be different from all the *other* kingdoms, and it will devour the whole earth and tread it down and crush it.
2. As for the ten horns, out of this kingdom ten kings will arise; and another will arise after them, and he will be different from the previous ones and will subdue three kings"
3. And he will speak out against the Most High and wear down the saints of the Highest One,[19] and he will intend to make alterations in times and in law; and they will be given into his hand for a time, times, and half a time.
4. But the court will sit *for judgment*, and his dominion will be taken away, annihilated and destroyed forever.
5. Then the sovereignty, the dominion, and the greatness of *all* the kingdoms under the whole heaven will be given to the people of the saints of the Highest One; His kingdom *will be* an everlasting kingdom, and all the dominions will serve and obey Him" (Dan 7:23-27).

There are several facts that can be gleaned from Daniel's vision of the fourth beast. The fourth beast will be a fourth kingdom on the earth. This kingdom will be totally different from all the previous kingdoms. This kingdom will devour the whole earth and crush it. This is speaking of a global take over by this final gentile world kingdom or empire.

As for the ten horns, out of this final or fourth gentile kingdom ten kings will come to power. There will be another horn or king who will arise after them. This king will be completely different from the previous kings and will subdue[20]

---

[19]The saints here are the remnant of Israel during the last half of the 70th week of Daniel known also as the time of great tribulation.

[20]שְׁפַל verb... *bring low, humble*...Dan. 5:22 *thou hast* not *humbled thine heart*[20] Francis Brown, Samuel Rolles Driver and Charles Augustus Briggs, *Enhanced Brown-Driver-Briggs Hebrew and English Lexicon*, electronic ed. (Oak Harbor, WA: Logos Research Systems, 2000), 1117. [UBS] ταπεινόω humble; make ashamed, humiliate; [Friberg] ταπεινόω ... literally *lower,*

three kings. He will speak out against the Most High and wear down the saints of the Highest One and he will make alterations in times and in law; and they will be given into his hand for a time, times, and half a time.[21] But the court will judge, and his dominion will be taken away, annihilated and destroyed forever. Then the sovereignty, the dominion, and the greatness of *all* the kingdoms under the whole heaven will be given to the people of the saints of the Highest One; His kingdom *will be* an everlasting kingdom, and all the dominions will serve and obey Him.[22]

---

make low; …figuratively; (a) in a negative sense, of assigning someone or oneself to a lower place in order to abase *humiliate, humble, degrade*; [Liddell-Scott] ταπεινόω … *to humble, abase*.... This king will somehow bring 3 of the 10 kings under his control. The ruler is the anti-christ nicknamed this by John in 1ˢᵗ and 2ⁿᵈ John.

[21]"Besides several facts already given about this coming king… three additional ones are now revealed: (1) He will oppose God's authority. He will speak against the Most High… (2) He will oppress His saints (i.e., Israel…)(3) He will introduce an entirely new era in which he will abandon all previous laws and institute his own system. As in 9:27a, he will appear as Israel's friend, but will become Israel's persecutor (the saints will be handed over to him) and he will occupy Jerusalem as the capital of his empire (11:45) for three and one-half years (Rev. 12:6; 13:5). A time, times, and half a time (cf. Dan. 12:7; Rev. 12:14) refer to the three and one-half years of the Great Tribulation, with "a time" meaning one year, "times" two years, and "half a time" six months. This equals the 1,260 days in Revelation 12:6 and the 42 months in Revelation 11:2; 13." J. Dwight Pentecost, "Daniel" In , in *The Bible Knowledge Commentary: An Exposition of the Scriptures*, ed. J. F. Walvoord and R. B. Zuck (Wheaton, IL: Victor Books, 1985), Dan. 7:25.

[22]The interpretation of Dan. 7:15-28: "The saints of the Most High' who 'receive the kingdom… are the saved Jewish remnant who pass through the Great Tribulation and inherit the kingdom and the covenants and promises made to Israel in connection with it. Note that the kingdom will be *eternal*… It is important that the designation of God as the Most High, possessor of heaven and earth (Gen 14:18–22), is used when the Messiah comes to make good that title in His kingdom rule, 27. It is essential to see that the 'fourth beast,' 23, and the ten-kingdom confederation growing out of it, 24, are *not* Macedonian Greece and Antiochus Epiphanes, 25–26, as critics commonly assert, but last-day revived Rome, since the whole context involves the *second* advent of Messiah and His subsequent rule." Merrill Frederick

Daniel's second vision of the ram and goat

Daniel was given a second vision providing more information of the times of the Gentiles. "In the third year of the reign of Belshazzar the king a vision appeared to me, Daniel, subsequent to the one which appeared to me previously. And I looked in the vision, and it came about while I was looking, that I was in the citadel of Susa... Then I lifted my gaze and looked, and behold, a **ram** which had two horns was standing in front of the canal... While I was observing, behold, a **male goat** was coming from the west over the surface of the whole earth without touching the ground; and the goat *had* a conspicuous horn between his eyes" (Dan 8:1-5)

Daniel was also given the interpretation of the ram and the goat. "And he said, Behold, I am going to let you know what will occur at the final period of the indignation, for *it* pertains to the appointed time of the end.

The ram which you saw with the two horns represents the kings of Media and Persia. And the **shaggy goat** *represents* **the kingdom of Greece**, and the **large horn** that is between his eyes **is the first king**" (Dan 8:19-21).

Daniel was given very detailed information with this vision. What was revealed to Daniel might look something like this:

- Ram – kings of Media and Persia
- Goat -- the kingdom of Greece
- Goat's horn -- the king of Greece

Daniel knew all this pertained to the future, but he did not fully understand all the visions with *all* the details revealed to him. "Then I, Daniel, was exhausted and sick for days. Then

Unger, *The New Unger's Bible Handbook*, Rev. and updated ed. (Chicago: Moody Publishers, 2005), 314.

I got up *again* and carried on the king's business; but I was astounded at the vision, and there was none to explain *it*" (Dan 8:26-27).

There is a very real sense we can understand this better than Daniel as ages and kingdoms have passed which fit perfectly into all the visions presented in Daniel. Even the names of the kings and kingdoms are made quite clear. The purpose of all this is to define the final four kingdoms of the Gentiles during the times of the Gentiles.

As the fourth kingdom was not identified by name, in history this kingdom was and is Rome. All these kingdoms still exist in very subtle ways. Rome never died in any sense and will one day come back as the 10 toes of Nebuchadnezzar's vision and the terrifying beast or the fourth kingdom of Daniel's vision. Anti-christ will be the ruler of the final three and one half years of the 70th week of Daniel. So all these kingdoms have been fully identified and are known as the times of the Gentiles.

A summary of Nebuchadnezzar's vision and Daniel's visions

Nebuchadnezzar's vision (Dan. 2:1-49)

Head of gold – Nebuchadnezzar king of Babylon
Breast and arms of silver – another kingdom, inferior to Babylon
Belly and thighs of bronze – defined the 3rd kingdom
Legs of iron – defined as the 4th kingdom
Feet partly of iron and clay -- final form of 4th kingdom

Daniel's vision one (Dan. 7:1-28)
    Lion -- king 1
    Bear -- king 2
    Leopard -- king 3
    Terrifying beast -- king 4

Daniel's vision two (Dan. 8:1-26)
    Ram – kings of Media and Persia
    Goat -- the kingdom of Greece
    Goat's horn -- the king of Greece

Defining the kingdoms and kings in the times of the Gentiles

Head of gold – Nebuchadnezzar -- Lion -- king 1 -- Babylon

Breast and arms of silver – Bear -- king 2 -- Ram – Media and
                                                  Persia

Belly and thighs of bronze – Leopard -- king 3 -- Goat -- Greece
                                            Goat's horn
                                      (king of Greece)
Legs of iron – Terrifying beast -- king 4 -- Rome

Nebuchadnezzar's vision	Daniel's vision one	Daniel's vision two
Head of gold – Nebuchadnezzar, king of Babylon	Lion – king 1	
Breast and arms of silver	Bear -- king/s 2	Ram – kings of Media and Persia
Belly and thighs of bronze	Leopard – king 3	Goat -- the kingdom of Greece Goat's horn -- the king of Greece
Legs of iron and feet and 10 toes	Terrifying beast – king 4	

Conclusion

Because of all the idolatry and other evil, the covenanted throne and kingdom was removed from Israel. Because of the eternal nature of the covenants establishing the eternal throne and kingdom, they cannot be removed permanently. A rule or kingdom was given to the Gentiles beginning with Nebuchadnezzar king of Babylon (Jer. 27:5-8). This began 'the times of the Gentiles' which have been thoroughly discussed.

Until the times of the Gentiles ends there are no covenanted kingdoms on this planet except those of the Gentiles which are not covenanted by God in any sense.

In Luke 21:5-36, Christ presented an apocalyptic discourse concerning His second coming. There would be great tribulation and persecution of Israel and the continuous trampling down of Jerusalem until the times of the Gentiles be fulfilled (21:17-24). "Woe to those who are with child and to those who nurse babes in those days; for there will be great distress upon the land, and wrath to this people, and they will fall by the edge of the sword, and will be led captive into all the nations; and Jerusalem will be trampled[23] under foot by the Gentiles until the times of the Gentiles be fulfilled" (Luke 21:23-24).

From Christ's first coming until now, the earth is still in this time described biblically by Christ Himself as the times of the Gentiles.

---

[23]"Woe to those who are with child and to those who nurse babes in those days; for there will be great distress upon the land, and wrath to this people (Israel), and they (Israel) will fall by the edge of the sword, and will be led captive into all the nations; and Jerusalem will be **trampled** under foot by the Gentiles until the times of the Gentiles be fulfilled" (Luke 21:23-24) οὐαὶ ταῖς ἐν γαστρὶ ἐχούσαις καὶ ταῖς θηλαζούσαις ἐν ἐκείναις ταῖς ἡμέραις· ἔσται γὰρ ἀνάγκη μεγάλη ἐπὶ τῆς γῆς καὶ ὀργὴ τῷ λαῷ τούτῳ, 24 καὶ πεσοῦνται στόματι μαχαίρης καὶ αἰχμαλωτισθήσονται εἰς τὰ ἔθνη πάντα, καὶ Ἰερουσαλὴμ ἔσται **πατουμένη** ὑπὸ ἐθνῶν, ἄχρι οὗ πληρωθῶσιν καιροὶ ἐθνῶν. **πατουμένη** verb participle present passive nominative feminine singular from **πατέω** [UBS] ...trans. trample; [Friberg] ...transitively *tread, trample* something; in a hostile sense *tread down, trample*; figuratively *subdue by force, plunder, treat contemptuously* (LU 21.24). The present active participle represents a continuous plundering of Jerusalem. This has happened and will happen until the second coming of Jesus Christ to subdue all hostility and take His covenanted Davidic throne as the legitimate Son of David, the direct Heir Apparent to the throne and kingdom over Israel in Jerusalem.

Chapter 10
His kingdom was near but *never* here

The covenanted kingdom was offered to Israel

John the Baptist came as a forerunner of the King and His kingdom. He was announcing that the kingdom of God was near. "Now in those days John the Baptist came, preaching in the wilderness of Judea, saying, repent, for <u>the kingdom of heaven is at hand</u> for this is the one referred to by Isaiah the prophet,[1] saying, the voice of one crying in the wilderness, make ready the way of the Lord, make His paths straight!" (Mat. 3:1-3). He was not Elijah who yet is to come in the day of the Lord. [2]

Then Jesus, the covenanted King of the kingdom, appeared preaching the same message as John that the kingdom of heaven was at hand. He came to announce the good news that Israel's Davidic King and kingdom were being offered to Israel. "From that time <u>Jesus</u> began to preach and say, repent, for <u>the kingdom of heaven is at hand</u>" (Mat. 4:17). He was sent to the covenanted nation for the very purpose of preaching the kingdom of God. He made this very clear to everyone around Him that the kingdom of heaven was near. "But He said to them, <u>I must preach the kingdom of God to the other cities also, for I was sent for this purpose.</u> And He kept on preaching in the synagogues of Judea" (Luke 4:43-44).

John the Baptist, Jesus, and His disciples all preached the same message. The gospel of the kingdom of heaven or the kingdom of God was near or at hand.

---

[1]"A voice is calling, clear the way for the LORD in the wilderness; make smooth in the desert a highway for our God" (Isa. 40:3).
[2]"And they asked him, "what then? Are you Elijah?" And he said, I am not. Are you the Prophet? And he answered, No" (John 1:21). "Behold, I am going to send you Elijah the prophet before the coming of the great and terrible day of the LORD" (Mal. 4:5).

- "Now in those days <u>John the Baptist</u> came, preaching in the wilderness of Judea, saying, Repent, for <u>the kingdom of heaven is at hand</u>" (Mat. 3:1-2).
- "From that time <u>Jesus</u> began to preach and say, Repent, for <u>the kingdom of heaven is at hand</u>" (Mat. 4:17).
- "These <u>twelve</u> Jesus sent out after instructing them, saying, Do not go in *the* way of *the* Gentiles, and do not enter *any* city of the Samaritans; but rather go to the lost sheep of the house of Israel. And as you go, preach, saying, <u>the kingdom of heaven is at hand</u>" (Mat. 10:5-7).
- "And after John had been taken into custody, Jesus came into Galilee, preaching the gospel of God, and saying, The time is fulfilled, and the <u>kingdom of God is at hand</u>; repent and believe in the gospel" (Mark 1:14-15).
- "Now after this <u>the Lord appointed seventy others,</u> and sent them two and two ahead of Him to every city and place where He Himself was going to come... and heal those in it who are sick, <u>and say to them,</u> <u>the kingdom of God has come near to you.</u>" (Luke 10:1, 9).

All Israel needed to do was believe the gospel of their King and kingdom. The good news of the King and His kingdom was literally being offered to the nation Israel. Their King was literally here, however the kingdom was near but not here. Note there was never a message given by anyone that the King was 'near or at hand.' The King was here, yet the kingdom was 'near.'

All Israel had to do was believe Him. No promises, no commitments as all the promises had been eternally made or covenanted unconditionally by God with His people Israel. God swore by His holiness that He would carry out exactly what He covenanted with David.[3] He is going to carry out His literal Word, Word for Word.

---

[3]"My covenant I will not violate, nor will I alter the utterance of My lips. Once I have sworn by My holiness; I will not lie to David. His descendants shall endure forever, and his throne as the sun before Me. It shall be

Jesus' message and John's message

As has been previously shown, there is only one kingdom. John the Baptist, Jesus, and His disciples preached identically the same message. They consistently preached the kingdom was near in that it was literally being offered to Israel. The Messiah, the King of Israel, the King of the kingdom was here, but the kingdom was not.   Note that the phrase 'the kingdom of heaven is at hand' used by John and Jesus are identical. Not only is the main verb identical ἤγγικεν,[4] every word in the Greek Text for this phrase is identical. This is very significant as there is only one kingdom being offered to the nation Israel. The kingdom was never modified or changed into multiple kingdoms.

- "Now in those days <u>John the Baptist</u> came, preaching in the wilderness of Judea, saying, Repent, for **the kingdom of heaven is at hand**" (Mat. 3:1-2). Ἐν δὲ ταῖς ἡμέραις ἐκείναις παραγίνεται Ἰωάννης ὁ βαπτιστὴς κηρύσσων ἐν τῇ ἐρήμῳ τῆς Ἰουδαίας ² [καὶ] λέγων· <u>μετανοεῖτε· ἤγγικεν γὰρ ἡ βασιλεία τῶν οὐρανῶν.</u>

- "From that time <u>Jesus</u> began to preach and say, Repent, for **the kingdom of heaven is at hand**" (Mat. 4:17). Ἀπὸ τότε ἤρξατο ὁ Ἰησοῦς κηρύσσειν καὶ λέγειν· <u>μετανοεῖτε· ἤγγικεν γὰρ ἡ βασιλεία τῶν οὐρανῶν.</u>

- <u>μετανοεῖτε· ἤγγικεν γὰρ ἡ βασιλεία τῶν οὐρανῶν. (John's message)</u>
- <u>μετανοεῖτε· ἤγγικεν γὰρ ἡ βασιλεία τῶν οὐρανῶν. (Jesus' message)</u>

---

established forever like the moon, and the witness in the sky is faithful" (Ps. 89:34-37).

[4] The main verb ἤγγικεν 'is at hand' is a perfect indicative in both verses used by John and Jesus. Again they both had identical messages.

Israel was to repent or change its mind about their King and His kingdom, literally 'only believe' i.e. they were to believe Him. With the rejection of the true Messiah came also the rejection of His kingdom. As Israel rejected their covenanted King, at the same time they also rejected the covenanted kingdom. They go literally hand in hand. There is no covenanted kingdom without the covenanted King. Israel must accept the very Person of Christ and exactly Who He is by covenanted design of the Designer.

1. "For <u>a child will be born to us</u>, a <u>Son will be given to us</u>;
2. And the government will rest on His shoulders;
3. And His name will be called <u>Wonderful Counselor, Mighty God, Eternal Father, Prince of Peace</u>.
4. There will be no end to the increase of *His* government or of peace,
5. <u>On the throne of David and over his kingdom</u>,
6. To establish it and to uphold it <u>with justice and righteousness from then on and forevermore</u>.
7. <u>The zeal of the LORD of hosts will accomplish this</u>" (Isa 9:6-7).

Man cannot build this kingdom, only God. Only God can accomplish all He has covenanted for His covenants are eternal, unilateral, and unconditional. His eternal covenants were cut exclusively with the nation Israel. All they had to do was believe the Son, the eternal Son of God.

- Jesus is the Eternal Son of God (Eternal Son given)
- Jesus is the Son of David (Son born of David, proper lineage)
- Jesus is the legitimate Heir Apparent to the covenanted throne

- Jesus is the legitimate Heir Apparent to the covenanted kingdom
- Jesus is the King of Israel
- Jesus is the King of the covenanted Davidic kingdom
- Jesus is the Christ, Israel's Messiah

Israel rejected the forerunner of their King as well as their King. The kingdom had not come in any sense with John the Baptist any more than it did with Jesus. The kingdom was near but never here. Their covenanted King had come. The covenanted kingdom had come upon Israel in the presence of their covenanted King, but they did not want His forerunner, Him, or His kingdom. They should have recognized the time of their visitation.

The kingdom offer was removed

Israel rejected their King and kingdom. The offer of the kingdom was finally and fully removed by Christ Himself. "Therefore I say to you, the kingdom of God will be taken away from you, and be given to a nation producing the fruit of it" (Mat 21:43). This verse seems to present several issues yet there is nothing difficult here.

The covenanted 'kingdom of God' was covenanted eternally with one people and that is the nation Israel. This was not only unconditional, but eternal, and unilateral. It is totally dependent on God to carry out His kingdom program with Israel. God has sworn by His own holiness, He will carry out every jot and tittle promised to David. God's very nature is on the proverbial line. What seems to be the issue is the word 'nation.' What nation is He referring to other than Israel? There is no other nation other than Israel to whom the throne and kingdom can be given. It cannot be given to the Gentiles, the church, or any other people for God has eternally covenanted this kingdom with His only covenanted nation which is Israel. This cannot change "for the gifts and the calling of God are irrevocable" (Rom. 11:29).

"Therefore I say to you, the kingdom of God will be taken away from you, and be given to a <u>nation</u> producing the fruit of it" (Mat 21:43). The basic meaning of the word nation ἔθνος[5] is generally a people group, a number of people as a company, body of men, a special class, a caste, a generation and several other related meanings. With the article, it usually means non-Jews. Jesus did not say to Israel or the leaders of Israel 'the kingdom of God will be taken away from you and be given to another nation, i.e. the Gentiles, the church, or any other people. There is not even a hint of this in the context. Also this would be impossible based on the nature of the eternal covenants and the nature of God. There will never be a violation of His inerrant Word for it is His Word and He cannot err. This would be a direct violation of His covenants i.e. quite literally His Word.

"A better interpretation is that Jesus was simply saying the kingdom was being taken away from the nation Israel at that time, but it would be given back to the nation in a future day when that nation would demonstrate true repentance and faith. In this view Jesus was using the term "nation" in the sense of generation (cf. Matt. 23:36). Because of their rejection, that generation of Israel would never be able to experience the kingdom of God... But a future generation in Israel will respond in saving faith to this same Messiah (Rom. 11:26–27),

---

[5][UBS] ἔθνος, ους n nation, people; τὰ ἔ. non-Jews, Gentiles; pagans, heathen, unbelievers; [Friberg]…generally *nation, people* (LU 7.5); (2) plural τὰ ἔθνη used to designate non-Jews *Gentiles, nations, foreigners* (RO 15.10, 11), opposite λαός (*people*); in a negative sense *pagans, heathen* (MT 6.32); [Liddell-Scott] … *a number of people accustomed to live together, a company, body of men;… a special class* of men, *a caste, tribe;* [Thayer] **1.** *a multitude* (whether of men or of beasts) *associated or living together; a company, troop, swarm…* **2.** A multitude of individuals of the same nature or genus; (BDAG) a body of persons united by kinship, culture, and common traditions, *nation, people, …* In Mt 21:43 ἔ. (not gentiles) in contrast to the leaders described vv. 23; 45. William Arndt, Frederick W. Danker and Walter Bauer, *A Greek-English Lexicon of the New Testament and Other Early Christian Literature*, 3rd ed. (Chicago: University of Chicago Press, 2000), 276-77.

and to that future generation the kingdom will be given. By rejecting Jesus the Stone, these builders (Matt. 21:42) suffered judgment (he on whom it [the Stone] falls will be crushed). The religious leaders (then the chief priests and the Pharisees, v. 45; cf. v. 23) realized Jesus' remarks were directed toward them, and they tried their best to arrest Him. But they were afraid of the ... people (cf. v. 26), who thought Jesus was a Prophet (cf. v. 11), so they were unable to act."[6]

Conclusion

John the Baptist, Jesus, and His disciples all preached the same message. The kingdom of God or Heaven was near. It was only near in the sense the King had come and was here. The people rejected the King and the kingdom. It was a legitimate offer, but Israel refused to believe Him. Jesus made one thing very clear: "O Jerusalem, Jerusalem, who kills the prophets and stones those who are sent to her! How often I wanted to gather your children together, the way a hen gathers her chicks under her wings, and you were unwilling. Behold, your house is being left to you desolate! For I say to you, from now on you shall not see Me until you say, Blessed is He who comes in the name of the Lord!" (Mat. 23:37-39).

In the day of the Lord, Israel will pray for His coming and their deliverance. "And it will come about that whoever calls on the name of the LORD Will be delivered" (Joel 2:32). "And thus all Israel will be saved; just as it is written, the Deliverer will come from Zion, He will remove ungodliness from Jacob" (Rom. 11:26).

---

[6] Louis A. Barbieri Jr., "Matthew" in *The Bible Knowledge Commentary: An Exposition of the Scriptures*, ed. J. F. Walvoord and R. B. Zuck (Wheaton, IL: Victor Books, 1985), Mt 21:40–46.

Chapter 11
The nature of His kingdom

There is a vast amount of information concerning the Lord's covenanted kingdom presented in His Word especially by the prophets. There are several issues which must be addressed which are an essential part to understand His coming kingdom.

The first area of importance which will be discussed is Christ's rule with justice and righteousness. This will be followed by Christ's rule with a rod of iron followed by Christ dwelling among men.

- Christ will rule with justice and righteousness
- Christ will rule with a rod of iron
- Christ will dwell among His people

God's Word was given primarily to reveal Himself as the Sovereign Creator to man. Man as a created being would know nothing of His love, mercy, grace, lovingkindness, justice, righteousness and many other wonderful things about the Creator unless He had revealed them to him.[1]

There are literally hundreds of verses which speak of all these wonderful blessings of the Lord and much more. However, the Lord has told man what He truly delights in and should not man delight in the same things?

- "But let him who boasts boast of this, that he understands and knows Me, that I am the LORD who exercises <u>lovingkindness, justice, and righteousness on earth; for I delight in these things declares the LORD</u>" (Jer. 9:24).

---

[1]All these things were to be a major focus of His earthly kingdom, and all these things will completely permeate His coming millennial reign. They all need to be fully studied and treasured.

- "He has told you, O man, what is good; and what does the LORD require of you <u>but to do justice, to love kindness, and to walk humbly with your God</u>" (Mic. 6:8).

- "The LORD is <u>good</u> to all, and His <u>mercies</u> are over all His works" (Ps. 145:9).

Man would know none of this unless it had been revealed by a just and loving Lord and Creator.

<u>"Righteousness and justice</u>
are the foundation of Thy
throne; Lovingkindness and
truth go before Thee" (Ps.
89:14).

The two major areas of focus presented here are justice and righteousness. Both these are necessary and vital truths of Christ's covenanted kingdom.

Christ will rule with justice and righteousness

During the days of His covenanted kingdom on the earth, His kings were to display justice and righteousness. "So David reigned over all Israel; and David administered <u>justice and righteousness for all his people</u>" (2 Sam. 8:15).

Solomon, his son, also did the same in his kingdom rule over Israel. "Blessed be the LORD your God who delighted in you to set you on the throne of Israel; because the LORD loved Israel forever, therefore He made you king, <u>to do justice and righteousness</u>" (1 King 10:9).

As justice and righteousness are the foundation of His throne, the Lord wanted justice and righteousness to literally flow from His eternal throne to the Davidic throne and kingdom to all men. It must be noted that God had adopted the earthly covenanted throne and kingdom as His very own.[2] "And of all my sons (for the LORD has given me many sons), He has chosen my son Solomon to sit on <u>the throne of the kingdom of the LORD over Israel</u>" (1 Chron. 28:5);

All men in the covenanted kingdom were also to display justice and righteousness. Not only is this truth the foundation of His throne, this truth was the very bedrock of the kingdom.

- "The LORD is exalted, for He dwells on high; He has filled Zion with <u>justice and righteousness</u>" (Is. 33:5).

- "Thus says the LORD, Do <u>justice and righteousness</u>, and deliver the one who has been robbed from the power of *his* oppressor. Also do not mistreat *or* do violence to the stranger, the orphan, or the widow; and do not shed innocent blood in this place" (Jer. 22:3).

---

[2]God adopted the Davidic throne and kingdom as His very own. This is why the earthly throne and kingdom is called by God, My house, My throne and My kingdom. "And it shall come about when your days are fulfilled that you must go *to be* with your fathers, that I will set up *one of* your descendants after you, who shall be of your sons; and I will establish his kingdom. He shall build for Me a house, and I will establish his throne forever. I will be his father, and he shall be My son; and I will not take My lovingkindness away from him, as I took it from him who was before you. But I will settle him in **My house and in My kingdom forever**, and his throne shall be established forever. According to all these words and according to all this vision, so Nathan spoke to David" (1 Chron. 17:11-15); "And of all my sons (for the LORD has given me many sons), He has chosen my son Solomon to sit on **the throne of the kingdom of the LORD over Israel**" (1 Chron. 28:5); **"Then Solomon sat on the throne of the LORD as king** instead of David his father; and he prospered, and all Israel obeyed him" (1 Chron. 29:23); "Blessed be the LORD your God who delighted in you, **setting you on His throne as king for the LORD your God**; because your God loved Israel establishing them forever, therefore He made you king over them, to do justice and righteousness" (2 Chron. 9:8); "So now you intend to resist **the kingdom of the LORD through the sons of David**, being a great multitude and *having* with you the golden calves which Jeroboam made for gods for you" (2 Chron. 13:8). For more information on this see George Peter's, *The Theocratic Kingdom*, proposition 35.

- "Yet you say, why should the son not bear the punishment for the father's iniquity?' When the son has practiced <u>justice and righteousness</u>, and has observed all My statutes and done them, he shall surely live" (Ezek. 18:19).

- "But if the wicked man turns from all his sins which he has committed and observes all My statutes and practices <u>justice and righteousness</u>, he shall surely live; he shall not die" (Ezek. 18:21).

- "Again, when a wicked man turns away from his wickedness which he has committed and practices <u>justice and righteousness</u>, he will save his life" (Ezek. 18:27).

The Lord wanted Solomon's kingdom on earth to be fully identified with justice and righteousness. Justice and righteousness may be simply defined by what God requires. If man did what delights God, then all would be right or just with God.   This would include all truth revealed to man about God by His Word.

Israel as His earthly kingdom represented Him as His kingdom of priests. Again His kingdom was to be virtually indwelt by His justice and righteousness. But all this fell abysmally short of what God wanted and delighted in.

"Thus says the LORD, "Go down to the house of the king of Judah, and there speak this word, and say,

1. 'Hear the word of the LORD, O king of Judah, who sits on David's throne, you and your servants and your people who enter these gates.

2. Thus says the LORD, <u>do justice and righteousness</u>,

3. And deliver the one who has been robbed
   from the power of *his* oppressor.
4. Also do not mistreat *or* do violence to the
   stranger, the orphan, or the widow;
5. And do not shed innocent blood in this place.
6. For if you men will indeed perform this
   thing, then kings will enter the gates of this
   house, sitting in David's place on his throne,
   riding in chariots and on horses, *even the
   king* himself and his servants and his people.
7. But if you will not obey these words, I swear
   by Myself, declares the LORD, that this
   house will become a desolation" (Jer. 22:1-
   5).

The covenanted throne was taken away[3] for a season but
it will be restored only by Him, the Lord Jesus Christ. But
observe carefully what He will do.

- "Behold, *the* days are coming, declares the LORD,
  When I shall raise up for David a righteous Branch; And
  He will reign as king and act wisely And do justice and
  righteousness in the land" (Jer. 23:5).

- "In those days and at that time I will cause a righteous
  Branch of David to spring forth; and He shall execute
  justice and righteousness on the earth" (Jer. 33:15)

- "There will be no end to the increase of *His* government
  or of peace, on the throne of David and over his
  kingdom, to establish it and to uphold it with justice and

---

[3]"If his sons forsake My law, And do not walk in My judgments, If they
violate My statutes, And do not keep My commandments, Then I will visit
their transgression with the rod, And their iniquity with stripes" (Ps 89:30-
32)

righteousness From then on and forevermore. The zeal of the LORD of hosts will accomplish this" (Is. 9:7).

- "Then all your people *will be* righteous; they will possess the land forever, The branch of My planting, The work of My hands, That I may be glorified" (Is. 60:21).

None of this is happening today. This has never happened in the church or church age. All this totally ceased when the times of the Gentiles began. This is why we are to seek and pray for that wonderful time when He will truly rule with mercy and grace from His covenanted throne in Jerusalem. There is no kingdom like this today in any sense. While men may create their own kingdoms with their imaginations as that of a Davidic throne in heaven, men are to seek His kingdom defined by justice and righteousness which will flow from the covenanted Davidic throne in Jerusalem. This will only happen when Jesus, Israel's Messiah reigns. Justice and righteousness will reign supreme in the greatness of Christ's kingdom.

- "There will be no end to the increase of *His* government or of peace, on the throne of David and over his kingdom, to establish it and to uphold it with justice and righteousness From then on and forevermore. The zeal of the LORD of hosts will accomplish this" (Is. 9:7).

- "But seek first His kingdom and His righteousness; and all these things shall be added to you" (Mat. 6:33).

There is no earthly kingdom without His justice and righteousness flowing in all the earth. When He returns and takes His covenanted throne over Israel, only then will justice and righteousness prevail in Israel and on the entire planet. This can only happen when the King of peace is ruling from His covenanted Davidic throne. Then it can be truly said:

"But let justice roll down like
waters And righteousness like
an ever-flowing stream"
(Amos 5:24)

Christ will rule with a rod of iron

Psalm two reveals Messiah's kingship and kingdom.
This was a royal psalm describing the Lord, the nations, and the
rule of the Davidic king. It shows how the nations were taking
a stand against the Lord and His anointed, the Davidic king.
Yet God is not mocked by this foolishness, for His King will
rule. The Lord will eventually place His Son upon the Davidic
throne and He will break the nations with a rod of iron. This
means He will put down all rebellion against Him, His
kingdom, His reign, and ultimately the Lord. He will then rule
the nations with a rod of iron.

Psalm two tells this whole story or age until Christ is
reigning on the earth. "This previews Christ's present rejection,
1–3 (cf. Acts 4:25–28), which continues throughout this age and
culminates in the abysmal apostasy of the Great Tribulation.
Messiah's attitude of disdain toward His enemies and His future
throne are foretold, 4–6. The future incarnate and risen Lord (cf.
Acts 13:33–34) vindicates His sonship at His second advent and
assumes the kingdom, 7–9. He exhorts kings and warns rebels
in view of the establishment of His kingdom, 10–12."[4]

1. "Why are the nations in an uproar, and the
    peoples devising a vain thing? The kings of
    the earth take their stand, and the rulers take
    counsel together Against the LORD and
    against His Anointed: Let us tear their fetters
    apart, and cast away their cords from us! (1-
    3)

---

[4]Merrill Frederick Unger, *The New Unger's Bible Handbook*, Rev. and
updated ed. (Chicago: Moody Publishers, 2005), 233.

2. <u>He who sits in the heavens laughs, The Lord scoffs at them</u>. Then He will speak to them in His anger and terrify them in His fury: But as for Me<u>, I have installed My King Upon Zion, My holy mountain. (4-6)</u>

3. I will surely tell of the decree of the LORD: He said to Me, Thou art My Son, Today I have begotten Thee. <u>Ask of Me, and I will surely give the nations as Thine inheritance, And the *very* ends of the earth as Thy possession. Thou shalt break them with a rod of iron, Thou shalt shatter them like earthenware. (7-9)</u>

4. <u>Now therefore, O kings, show discernment; Take warning, O judges of the earth. Worship the LORD with reverence, and rejoice with trembling. Do homage to the Son, lest He become angry, and you perish *in* the way, For His wrath may soon be kindled.</u> How blessed are all who take refuge in Him!" (10-12) (Ps. 2:1-12).

Christ will take control of the nations in the day of the Lord at His second coming. He will first smite the nations with His wrath, cause all rebellion to cease, and then take full control of the nations through the Davidic throne. Then it can be said "I will surely give the nations as Thine inheritance, and the *very* ends of the earth as Thy possession. Thou shalt break them with a rod of iron, Thou shalt shatter them like earthenware." All this is so important to realize for this has not and is not happening today during the times of the Gentiles.

- <u>And he shall rule them with a rod of iron</u>, as the vessels of the potter are broken to pieces, as I also have received *authority* from My Father" (Rev. 2:27).

- "And she gave birth to a son, a male *child*, who is to rule all the nations with a rod of iron; and her child was caught up to God and to His throne" (Rev. 12:5).

- "And from His mouth comes a sharp sword, so that with it He may smite the nations; and He will rule them with a rod of iron; and He treads the wine press of the fierce wrath of God, the Almighty" (Rev. 19:15).

There is no kingdom on the planet which represents anything like this. As part of the greatness of His reign and kingdom, He will rule sovereignly but with justice and righteousness.

Christ will dwell among His people
God has cherished dwelling among His people. He has shown this in so many ways. This is a wonderful truth of His kingdom reign, when Christ dwells among His people.

From the beginning there was a desire of the Lord to dwell among men. This can be seen with Adam and his relationship with the Lord prior to sin. The Lord and man seemed to enjoy personal fellowship. "And they heard the sound of the LORD God walking in the garden in the cool of the day, and the man and his wife hid themselves from the presence of the LORD God among the trees of the garden" (Gen 3:8). The fact was the LORD God was 'walking in the garden in the cool of the day.' It appears He was looking for Adam, and possibly this was a normal occurrence at least for a season. There is nothing in the Text to indicate otherwise. Yet after man's sin, man and woman hid themselves from the One Who not only created them, but wished to visit with them. "The effects of sin are punishment and provision. Whereas **the man** and the woman had life, they now had death; whereas pleasure, now pain; whereas abundance, now a meager subsistence by toil; whereas perfect fellowship, now alienation and conflict."[5]

God's dwelling place with Israel

God made it very clear to the nation Israel that He is to dwell among them. They are His covenanted people and He will carry out every detail of His eternal covenants with them. His very presence with them proves His love for Israel by just wanting to dwell among them. He was proving He was their God, and wanted to be their God by demonstrating this by His very presence. "God, whose true dwelling place is beyond the heavens, desired a structure that would represent His holy presence among His people. That I may dwell is related to the Hebrew verb from which we derive the word Shekinah, which designates the radiance, glory, and presence of God dwelling among His people."[6]

- "And let them construct a sanctuary for Me, <u>that I may dwell among them</u>" (Ex. 25:8).

- "<u>And I will dwell among the sons of Israel and will be their God</u>" (Ex. 29:45).

- "And they shall know that I am the LORD their God who brought them out of the land of Egypt, <u>that I might dwell among them; I am the LORD their God</u>" (Ex. 29:46).

- "You shall send away both male and female; you shall send them outside the camp so that they will not defile their camp <u>where I dwell in their midst</u>" (Num. 5:3).

---

[5]Allen P. Ross, "Genesis" in *The Bible Knowledge Commentary: An Exposition of the Scriptures*, ed. J. F. Walvoord and R. B. Zuck (Wheaton, IL: Victor Books, 1985), Gen. 3:8–13.
[6]*The Nelson Study Bible*, Earl Radmacher, General Editor (Nashville, Thomas Nelson Publishers, 1997), 143.

- "And you shall not defile the land in which you live, <u>in the midst of which I dwell; for I the LORD am dwelling in the midst of the sons of Israel</u>" (Num. 35:34).

The Lord wanted to dwell among His people, the nation Israel. The people did not appreciate what they had in a wonderful and loving Lord. They sought other gods, and He departed. But one day He will dwell with them ruling from David's throne forever.

God indwelling the church

The dwelling of God on the earth is in the church. "The church is **the temple of God** (cf. 1 Cor. 3:16) where the Spirit of God and Christ dwells."[7] The church age began on the day of Pentecost with Spirit baptism, and the church ends at the rapture with the fullness of the Gentiles. "For I do not want you, brethren, to be uninformed of this mystery, lest you be wise in your own estimation, that a partial hardening has happened to Israel until the fullness of the Gentiles[8] has come in" (Rom. 11:25).

- "Or what agreement has the temple of God with idols? <u>For we are the temple of the living God; just as God said, I will dwell in them and walk among them</u>; and I will be their God, and they shall be My people" (2 Cor. 6:16).

- "So then you are no longer strangers and aliens, but you are fellow citizens with the saints, and are of God's

---

[7] David K. Lowery, "2 Corinthians" In , in *The Bible Knowledge Commentary: An Exposition of the Scriptures*, ed. J. F. Walvoord and R. B. Zuck (Wheaton, IL: Victor Books, 1985), 2 Co 6:16.

[8] The fullness of the Gentiles is not the times of the Gentiles. The times of the Gentiles have already been defined as when there is no ruling monarch or king on David's throne. The fullness of the Gentiles is when the last Gentile is saved, this will end the church age.

household, having been built upon the foundation of the apostles and prophets, Christ Jesus Himself being the corner *stone*, in whom the whole building, being fitted together is growing into a holy temple in the Lord; <u>in whom you also are being built together into a dwelling of God in the Spirit</u>" (Eph 2:19-22).

- "<u>So that Christ may dwell in your hearts through faith;</u> *and* that you, being rooted and grounded in love" (Eph. 3:17).

There is a true sense that Christ is dwelling in the church as a temple. Israel was never called or addressed as a temple of God as the church. However He will dwell among Israel in His covenanted kingdom quite literally. "Gentile believers, are no longer foreigners (*xenoi;* cf. v. 12) and aliens. Believing Gentiles become fellow citizens with God's people and members of God's household. They become a part of the company of the redeemed of all ages beginning with Adam. However, this does not mean that the church inherits the blessings promised to Israel... Paul described the church as a great building, a holy temple in which God dwells."[9]

It must be noted that Christ's view of the church up to the writing of Revelation, the seven churches of Asia, was not very encouraging. The Lord rebuked at least five of His seven churches for departing from various truths (Rev. 2-3). Christ is found standing outside of one of the churches (Rev. 3:20). Paul warned of continued apostasy in the latter days of the church age (1 Tim. 4:1-2; 2 Tim. 3:1-9), and there are many other examples of departure from the truth or apostasy. As the church continues until the rapture, there appears to be a great departure from the truth that He is indwelling the believers as His temple.

---

[9] Harold W. Hoehner, "Ephesians" In , in *The Bible Knowledge Commentary: An Exposition of the Scriptures*, ed. J. F. Walvoord and R. B. Zuck (Wheaton, IL: Victor Books, 1985), Eph 2:19–20.

God's dwelling in the kingdom

In Christ's kingdom, He will dwell with His people. He will literally be among His covenanted people Israel. "And He said to me, Son of man, *this is* the place of My throne and the place of the soles of My feet, where I will dwell among the sons of Israel forever. And the house of Israel will not again defile My holy name, neither they nor their kings, by their harlotry and by the corpses of their kings when they die" (Ezek. 43:7). "God said the new temple is to be the place of His throne ... the place where He will live among the Israelites forever... The temple will serve as God's earthly dwelling place among His people. God assured Ezekiel that this home would be permanent. Never again would Israel defile His holy name... by worshiping lifeless idols, bringing destruction on the nation (43:7–8)."[10]

God's dwelling in the eternal state

- "And I heard a loud voice from the throne, saying, Behold, the tabernacle of God is among men, and He shall dwell among them, and they shall be His people, and God Himself shall be among them" (Rev. 21:3).

It has been biblically shown that God has desired to live among His people. The people either don't want this or are indifferent to it. In every age, God has tried to dwell among men, and only in Christ's kingdom and the eternal state will this be realized. The Psalmist said this best.

- "Surely goodness and lovingkindness will follow me all the days of my life, and I will dwell in the house of the LORD forever" (Ps. 23:6).

---

[10] Charles H. Dyer, "Ezekiel" In , in *The Bible Knowledge Commentary: An Exposition of the Scriptures*, ed. J. F. Walvoord and R. B. Zuck (Wheaton, IL: Victor Books, 1985), Eze 43:6–9.

As the Lord wished to dwell with His people, His people should have the same desire to live forever with Him. That is what eternal life is all about, that is just being with Him and enjoying Him forever. That is what makes heaven truly heaven. It is heaven because He is there.

Conclusion

There is a vast amount of information concerning the Lord's covenanted kingdom. Several very significant areas have been addressed which are an essential part to understand His coming kingdom.

- Christ will rule with justice and righteousness
- Christ will rule with a rod of iron
- Christ will dwell among His people

The true nature of Christ's kingdom and the greatness of it must include all the above. As eternal life is all about Him i.e. Who He is, and what He did,[11] Christ's kingdom and the greatness of it, is also all about Him. He said seek first the kingdom of God and His righteousness and all these things will be added to you.

He is the Eternal Son and the Son of David. He is the Heir Apparent to the covenanted Davidic throne. He will rule with perfect justice and righteousness. "He loves righteousness and justice; the earth is full of the lovingkindness of the LORD" (Ps. 33:5).

---

[11]He is the eternal Son of God, and He died for our sin and was raised from the dead on the 3rd day, it is all about Him. All we do is believe i.e. no promises and no commitments. And we don't make Him Lord of our lives. He is LORD, He is the Eternal Son. If one believes, He is Lord of one's life already.

At the end of His millennial reign, when He has subdued all unrighteousness,[12] He will transfer the kingdom to the Father into the eternal state.

> "Then *comes* the end, when He delivers up the kingdom to the God and Father, when He has abolished all rule and all authority and power. For He must reign until He has put all His enemies under His feet" (1 Cor. 15:24).

This is how His throne, His kingdom, and His rule are forever, they are merged into the eternal state. The greatness of His kingdom is quite literally a taste of eternity. There are those who truly desire to be with Him forever, so come soon Lord Jesus and bring in your kingdom. The kingdom and eternal state are simply wonderful for He is there.

> "But seek first His kingdom and His righteousness; and all these things shall be added to you" (Mat 6:33)

---

[12]God created man in His own image and gave him a mandate to subdue the earth and rule over it. What Adam did not do, the last Adam not only does all what God had mandated but much more. "Then God said, Let Us make man in Our image, according to Our likeness; and let them rule over the fish of the sea and over the birds of the sky and over the cattle and over all the earth, and over every creeping thing that creeps on the earth. And God created man in His own image, in the image of God He created him; male and female He created them. And God blessed them; and God said to them, be fruitful and multiply, and fill the earth, and subdue it; and rule over the fish of the sea and over the birds of the sky, and over every living thing that moves on the earth" (Gen 1:26-28). Man abysmally failed in this mandate but the last Adam or the second man will accomplish what man was originally created to do and more. So also it is written, the first man, Adam, became a living soul. The last Adam *became* a life-giving spirit" (1 Corinthians 15:45). "The first man is from the earth, earthy; the second man is from heaven" (1 Cor. 15:47).

"One thing I have asked from the LORD,
that I shall seek: That I may dwell in the
house of the LORD all the days of my life,
to behold the beauty of the LORD, And to
meditate in His temple" (Ps. 27:4)

Appendix A 'the day of the Lord'

1) Isaiah 13:6 Wail, for the day of the LORD is near! It will come as destruction from the Almighty.
2) Isaiah 13:9 Behold, the day of the LORD is coming, Cruel, with fury and burning anger, To make the land a desolation; And He will exterminate its sinners from it.
3) Lamentations 2:22 Thou didst call as in the day of an appointed feast My terrors on every side; And there was no one who escaped or survived In the day of the LORD's anger. Those whom I bore and reared, My enemy annihilated them.
4) Ezekiel 13:5 You have not gone up into the breaches, nor did you build the wall around the house of Israel to stand in the battle on the day of the LORD.
5) Ezekiel 30:3 For the day is near, Even the day of the LORD is near; It will be a day of clouds, A time *of doom* for the nations.
6) Joel 1:15 Alas for the day! For the day of the LORD is near, And it will come as destruction from the Almighty.
7) Joel 2:1 Blow a trumpet in Zion, And sound an alarm on My holy mountain! Let all the inhabitants of the land tremble, For the day of the LORD is coming; Surely it is near,
8) Joel 2:11 And the LORD utters His voice before His army; surely His camp is very great, for strong is he who carries out His word. The day of the LORD is indeed great and very awesome, and who can endure it?
9) Joel 2:31 The sun will be turned into darkness, And the moon into blood, before the great and awesome day of the LORD comes.
10) Joel 3:14 Multitudes, multitudes in the valley of decision! For the day of the LORD is near in the valley of decision.
11) Amos 5:18 Alas, you who are longing for the day of the LORD, For what purpose *will* the day of the LORD *be* to you? It *will be* darkness and not light;
12) Amos 5:20 Will not the day of the LORD *be* darkness instead of light, Even gloom with no brightness in it?

13) Obadiah 1:15 For <u>the day of the LORD</u> draws near on all the nations. As you have done, it will be done to you. Your dealings will return on your own head.

14) Zephaniah 1:7 Be silent before the Lord God! For <u>the day of the LORD</u> is near, For the LORD has prepared a sacrifice, He has consecrated His guests.

15) Zephaniah 1:8 "Then it will come about on <u>the day of the LORD</u>'s sacrifice, That I will punish the princes, the king's sons, and all who clothe themselves with foreign garments.

16) Zephaniah 1:14 Near is <u>the great day of the LORD</u>, Near and coming very quickly; Listen, <u>the day of the LORD</u>! In it the warrior cries out bitterly.

17) Zephaniah 1:18 Neither their silver nor their gold Will be able to deliver them On <u>the day of the LORD</u>'s wrath; And all the earth will be devoured In the fire of His jealousy, For He will make a complete end, Indeed a terrifying one, Of all the inhabitants of the earth.

18) Zephaniah 2:2 Before the decree takes effect-- The day passes like the chaff-- Before the burning anger of the LORD comes upon you, Before <u>the day of the LORD</u>'s anger comes upon you.

19) Zephaniah 2:3 Seek the LORD, All you humble of the earth Who have carried out His ordinances; Seek righteousness, seek humility. Perhaps you will be hidden In <u>the day of the LORD</u>'s anger.

20) Malachi 4:5 "Behold, I am going to send you Elijah the prophet before the coming of <u>the great and terrible day of the LORD</u>.

21) Acts 2:20 'The sun shall be turned into darkness, And the moon into blood, Before <u>the great and glorious day of the Lord</u> shall come.

22) 1 Corinthians 5:5 I *have decided* to deliver such a one to Satan for the destruction of his flesh, that his spirit may be saved in <u>the day of the LORD</u> Jesus.

23) 1 Thessalonians 5:2 For you yourselves know full well that <u>the day of the LORD</u> will come just like a thief in the night.

24) 2 Thessalonians 2:2 that you may not be quickly shaken from your composure or be disturbed either by a spirit or a message or a letter as if from us, to the effect that <u>the day of the LORD</u> has come.

25) 2 Peter 3:10 But <u>the day of the LORD</u> will come like a thief, in which the heavens will pass away with a roar and the elements will be destroyed with intense heat, and the earth and its works will be burned up.

Appendix B 'that day and a day'

1) Isaiah 2:11 The proud look of man will be abased, And the loftiness of man will be humbled, And the LORD alone will be exalted in <u>that day</u>. *(in His kingdom)*

2) Isaiah 2:12 For the LORD of hosts will have **a day** *of reckoning* Against everyone who is proud and lofty, And against everyone who is lifted up, That he may be abased. *(in the judgments of the day of the Lord)*

3) Isaiah 2:17 And the pride of man will be humbled, And the loftiness of men will be abased, And the LORD alone will be exalted in <u>that day</u>. *(in His kingdom)*

4) Isaiah 2:20 In <u>that day</u> men will cast away to the moles and the bats their idols of silver and their idols of gold, which they made for themselves to worship *(in His kingdom)*

5) Isaiah 4:2 In <u>that day</u> the Branch of the LORD will be beautiful and glorious, and the fruit of the earth *will* be the pride and the adornment of the survivors of Israel. *(in His kingdom)*

6) Isaiah 11:10 Then it will come about in <u>that day</u> that the nations will resort to the root of Jesse, Who will stand as a signal for the peoples; and His resting place will be glorious. *(in His kingdom)*

7) Isaiah 12:1 Then you will say on <u>that day</u>, I will give thanks to Thee, O LORD; For although Thou wast angry with me, Thine anger is turned away, And Thou dost comfort me. *(in His kingdom)*

8) Isaiah 12:4 And in <u>that day</u> you will say, "Give thanks to the LORD, call on His name. Make known His deeds among the peoples; Make *them* remember that His name is exalted." *(in His kingdom)*

9) Isaiah 19:23 In <u>that day</u> there will be a highway from Egypt to Assyria, and the Assyrians will come into Egypt and the

Egyptians into Assyria, and the Egyptians will worship with the Assyrians. *(in His kingdom)*

10) Isaiah 19:24 In that day Israel will be the third *party* with Egypt and Assyria, a blessing in the midst of the earth, *(in His kingdom)*

11) Isaiah 24:21 So it will happen in that day, That the LORD will punish the host of heaven, on high, And the kings of the earth, on earth. *(in the judgments of the day of the Lord)*

12) Isaiah 25:9 And it will be said in that day, "Behold, this is our God for whom we have waited that He might save us. This is the LORD for whom we have waited; Let us rejoice and be glad in His salvation *(in His kingdom)*

13) Isaiah 26:1 In that day this song will be sung in the land of Judah: "We have a strong city; He sets up walls and ramparts for security. *(in His kingdom)*

14) Isaiah 27:1 In that day the LORD will punish Leviathan the fleeing serpent, With His fierce and great and mighty sword, Even Leviathan the twisted serpent; And He will kill the dragon who *lives* in the sea.*(in the judgments of the day of the Lord)*

15) Isaiah 27:2 In that day, A vineyard of wine, sing of it! *(in His kingdom)*

16) Isaiah 27:6 In **the days** to come Jacob will take root, Israel will blossom and sprout; And they will fill the whole world with fruit. *(in His kingdom)*

17) Isaiah 27:12 And it will come about in that day, that the LORD will start *His* threshing from the flowing stream of the Euphrates to the brook of Egypt; and you will be gathered up one by one, O sons of Israel. *(in His kingdom)*

18) Isaiah 27:13 It will come about also in that day that a great trumpet will be blown; and those who were perishing in the land of Assyria and who were scattered in the land of Egypt will come and worship the LORD in the holy mountain at Jerusalem *(in His kingdom)*

19) Isaiah 28:5 In that day the LORD of hosts will become a beautiful crown And a glorious diadem to the remnant of His people *(in His kingdom)*

20) Isaiah 31:7 For in that day every man will cast away his silver idols and his gold idols, which your hands have made as a sin *(in His kingdom)*

21) Ezekiel 29:21 On that day I shall make a horn sprout for the house of Israel, and I shall open your mouth in their midst. Then they will know that I am the LORD *(in His kingdom)*

22) Ezekiel 38:14 Therefore, prophesy, son of man, and say to Gog, Thus says the Lord God, On that day when My people Israel are living securely, will you not know *it? (in the judgments of the day of the Lord)*

23) Ezekiel 38:18 And it will come about on that day, when Gog comes against the land of Israel, declares the Lord God, that My fury will mount up in My anger *(in the judgments of the day of the Lord)*

24) Ezekiel 38:19 And in My zeal and in My blazing wrath I declare *that* on that day there will surely be a great earthquake in the land of Israel *(in the judgments of the day of the Lord)*

25) Ezekiel 39:11 And it will come about on that day that I shall give Gog a burial ground there in Israel, the valley of those who pass by east of the sea, and it will block off the passers-by. So they will bury Gog there with all his multitude, and they will call *it* the valley of Hamon-gog. *(in the judgments of the day of the Lord)*

26) Ezekiel 39:22 And the house of Israel will know that I am the LORD their God from that day onward. *(in the judgments of the day of the Lord and into His kingdom)*

27) Ezekiel 45:22 And on that day the prince shall provide for himself and all the people of the land a bull for a sin offering *(in His kingdom)*

28) Ezekiel 48:35 *The city shall be* 18,000 *cubits* round about; and the name of the city from *that day shall be*, The LORD is there *(in His kingdom)*

29) Hosea 2:16 And it will come about in that day, declares the LORD, That you will call Me Ishi And will no longer call Me Baali *(in His kingdom)*

30) Hosea 2:18 In that day I will also make a covenant for them with the beasts of the field, the birds of the sky, and the creeping things of the ground. And I will abolish the bow, the sword, and war from the land, and will make them lie down in safety *(in His kingdom)*

31) Hosea 2:21 And it will come about in that day that I will respond, declares the LORD. I will respond to the heavens, and they will respond to the earth *(in His kingdom)*

32) Joel 3:18 And it will come about in that day That the mountains will drip with sweet wine, And the hills will flow with milk, And all the brooks of Judah will flow with water; And a spring will go out from the house of the LORD, To water the valley of Shittim *(in His kingdom)*

33) Amos 9:11 In that day I will raise up the fallen booth of David, And wall up its breaches; I will also raise up its ruins, And rebuild it as in the days of old *(in His kingdom)*

34) Micah 5:10 And it will be in that day, declares the LORD, That I will cut off your horses from among you and destroy your chariots *(in the judgments of the day of the Lord)*

35) Micah 7:11 It *will be* a day for building your walls. On that day will your boundary be extended *(in His kingdom)*

36) Zephaniah 1:9 And I will punish on that day all who leap on the *temple* threshold, Who fill the house of their lord with violence and deceit *(in the judgments of the day of the Lord)*

37) Zephaniah 1:10 And on that day, declares the LORD, There will be the sound of a cry from the Fish Gate, A wail from the Second Quarter, And a loud crash from the hills *(in the judgments of the day of the Lord)*

38) Zephaniah 1:15 A day of wrath is that day, A day of trouble and distress, A day of destruction and desolation, A day of darkness and gloom, A day of clouds and thick darkness, *(in the judgments of the day of the Lord)*

39) Zephaniah 3:11 In that day you will feel no shame Because of all your deeds By which you have rebelled against Me; For then I will remove from your midst Your proud, exulting ones, And you will never again be haughty On My holy mountain *(in His kingdom)*

40) Zephaniah 3:16 In that day it will be said to Jerusalem: Do not be afraid, O Zion; Do not let your hands fall limp *(in His kingdom)*

41) Zechariah 2:11 And many nations will join themselves to the LORD in that day and will become My people. Then I will dwell in your midst, and you will know that the LORD of hosts has sent Me to you. *(in His kingdom)*

42) Zechariah 3:10 'In that day,' declares the LORD of hosts, 'every one of you will invite his neighbor to *sit* under *his* vine and under *his* fig tree *(in His kingdom)*

43) Zechariah 12:3 And it will come about in that day that I will make Jerusalem a heavy stone for all the peoples; all who lift it will be severely injured. And all the nations of the earth will be gathered against it *(in the judgments of the day of the Lord)*

44) Zechariah 12:4 In that day, declares the LORD, I will strike every horse with bewilderment, and his rider with madness. But I will watch over the house of Judah, while I strike every horse of the peoples with blindness *(in the judgments of the day of the Lord)*

45) Zechariah 12:6 In that day I will make the clans of Judah like a firepot among pieces of wood and a flaming torch among sheaves, so they will consume on the right hand and on the left all the surrounding peoples, while the inhabitants of Jerusalem again dwell on their own sites in Jerusalem *(in the judgments of the day of the Lord)*

46) Zechariah 12:8 In that day the LORD will defend the inhabitants of Jerusalem, and the one who is feeble among them in that day will be like David, and the house of David *will be* like God, like the angel of the LORD before them *(in the judgments of the day of the Lord)*

47) Zechariah 12:9-10 And it will come about in that day that I will set about to destroy all the nations that come against Jerusalem. And I will pour out on the house of David and on the inhabitants of Jerusalem, the Spirit of grace and of supplication, so that they will look on Me whom they have pierced; and they will mourn for Him, as one mourns for an only son, and they will weep bitterly over Him, like the bitter weeping over a first-born *(in the judgments of the day of the Lord)*

48) Zechariah 12:11 In that day there will be great mourning in Jerusalem, like the mourning of Hadadrimmon in the plain of Megiddo. *(in the judgments of the day of the Lord)*

49) Zechariah 13:1 In that day a fountain will be opened for the house of David and for the inhabitants of Jerusalem, for sin and for impurity. *(in the judgments of the day of the Lord)*

50) Zechariah 13:2 And it will come about in <u>that day,</u> declares the LORD of hosts, "that I will cut off the names of the idols from the land, and they will no longer be remembered; and I will also remove the prophets and the unclean spirit from the land *(in the judgments of the day of the Lord)*

51) Zechariah 13:4 Also it will come about in <u>that day</u> that the prophets will each be ashamed of his vision when he prophesies, and they will not put on a hairy robe in order to deceive *(in the judgments of the day of the Lord)*

52) Zechariah 14:4 And in <u>that day</u> His feet will stand on the Mount of Olives, which is in front of Jerusalem on the east; and the Mount of Olives will be split in its middle from east to west by a very large valley, so that half of the mountain will move toward the north and the other half toward the south. *(in the judgments of the day of the Lord)*

53) Zechariah 14:6 And it will come about in <u>that day</u> that there will be no light; the luminaries will dwindle. *(in the judgments of the day of the Lord)*

54) Zechariah 14:7 For it will be **a unique day** which is known to the LORD, neither day nor night, but it will come about that at evening time there will be light. *(in the judgments of the day of the Lord)*

55) Zechariah 14:8 And it will come about in <u>that day</u> that living waters will flow out of Jerusalem, half of them toward the eastern sea and the other half toward the western sea; it will be in summer as well as in winter. *(in His kingdom)*

56) Zechariah 14:9 And the LORD will be king over all the earth; in <u>that day</u> the LORD will be *the only* one, and His name *the only* one *(in His kingdom)*

57) Zechariah 14:13 And it will come about in <u>that day</u> that a great panic from the LORD will fall on them; and they will seize one another's hand, and the hand of one will be lifted against the hand of another. . *(in the judgments of the day of the Lord)*

58) Zechariah 14:20 In <u>that day</u> there will *be inscribed* on the bells of the horses, "HOLY TO THE LORD." And the cooking pots in the LORD's house will be like the bowls before the altar. *(in His kingdom)*

59) Zechariah 14:21 And every cooking pot in Jerusalem and in Judah will be holy to the LORD of hosts; and all who

sacrifice will come and take of them and boil in them. And there will no longer be a Canaanite in the house of the LORD of hosts in that day *(in His kingdom)*

60) Matthew 7:22 Many will say to Me on that day, 'Lord, Lord, did we not prophesy in Your name, and in Your name cast out demons, and in Your name perform many miracles? *(in His kingdom)*

61) Matthew 26:29 But I say to you, I will not drink of this fruit of the vine from now on until that day when I drink it new with you in My Father's kingdom *(in His kingdom)*

62) Mark 13:32 But of that day or hour no one knows, not even the angels in heaven, nor the Son, but the Father *alone (in the judgments of the day of the Lord)*

63) Mark 14:25 Truly I say to you, I shall never again drink of the fruit of the vine until that day when I drink it new in the kingdom of God *(in His kingdom)*

64) Luke 6:23 Be glad in that day, and leap *for joy*, for behold, your reward is great in heaven; for in the same way their fathers used to treat the prophets *(in His kingdom)*

65) Luke 17:31 On that day, let not the one who is on the housetop and whose goods are in the house go down to take them away; and likewise let not the one who is in the field turn back *(in the judgments of the day of the Lord)*

66) 2 Thessalonians 1:10 when He comes to be glorified in His saints on that day, and to be marveled at among all who have believed-- for our testimony to you was believed. *(in the judgments of the day of the Lord into His kingdom)*

Appendix C 'the day'

1) Isaiah 13:13 Therefore I shall make the heavens tremble, and the earth will be shaken from its place at the fury of the LORD of hosts in **the day** of His burning anger.

2) Isaiah 30:25 And on every lofty mountain and on every high hill there will be streams running with water on **the day** of the great slaughter, when the towers fall.

3) Isaiah 61:2 To proclaim the favorable year of the LORD, And **the day** of vengeance of our God; To comfort all who mourn,

4) Isaiah 63:4 For **the day** of vengeance was in My heart, And My year of redemption has come.

5) Ezekiel 30:2 Son of man, prophesy and say, 'Thus says the Lord God, Wail, 'Alas for **the day**!'

6) Ezekiel 36:33 Thus says the Lord God, On **the day** that I cleanse you from all your iniquities, I will cause the cities to be inhabited, and the waste places will be rebuilt.

7) Ezekiel 39:8 Behold, it is coming and it shall be done, declares the Lord God. That is **the day** of which I have spoken.

8) Ezekiel 39:13 Even all the people of the land will bury *them*; and it will be to their renown *on* **the day** that I glorify Myself, declares the Lord God.

9) Ezekiel 43:18 And He said to me, Son of man, thus says the Lord God, 'These are the statutes for the altar on **the day** it is built, to offer burnt offerings on it and to sprinkle blood on it.

10) Ezekiel 44:27 And on **the day** that he goes into the sanctuary, into the inner court to minister in the sanctuary, he shall offer his sin offering, declares the Lord God.

11) Ezekiel 46:1 Thus says the Lord God, The gate of the inner court facing east shall be shut the six working days; but it shall be opened on the sabbath day, and opened on **the day** of the new moon.

12) Ezekiel 46:6 And on **the day** of the new moon *he shall offer* a young bull without blemish, also six lambs and a ram, *which* shall be without blemish.

13) Zephaniah 2:2 Before the decree takes effect-- **The day** passes like the chaff-- Before the burning anger of the LORD comes upon you, Before 's anger comes upon you.

14) Zephaniah 3:8 Therefore, wait for Me, declares the LORD, For **the day** when I rise up to the prey. Indeed, My decision is to gather nations, To assemble kingdoms, To pour out on them My indignation, All

My burning anger; For all the earth will be devoured By the fire of My zeal.

15) Malachi 3:2 But who can endure **the day** of His coming? And who can stand when He appears? For He is like a refiner's fire and like fullers' soap.

16) Malachi 3:17 And they will be Mine, says the LORD of hosts, on **the day** that I prepare *My* own possession, and I will spare them as a man spares his own son who serves him.

17) Malachi 4:1 For behold, **the day** is coming, burning like a furnace; and all the arrogant and every evildoer will be chaff; and **the day** that is coming will set them ablaze, says the LORD of hosts, so that it will leave them neither root nor branch.

18) Malachi 4:3 And you will tread down the wicked, for they shall be ashes under the soles of your feet on **the day** which I am preparing, says the LORD of hosts.

19) Matthew 10:15 Truly I say to you, it will be more tolerable for *the* land of Sodom and Gomorrah in **the day** of judgment, than for that city.

20) Matthew 11:22 Nevertheless I say to you, it shall be more tolerable for Tyre and Sidon in **the day** of judgment, than for you.

21) Matthew 11:24 Nevertheless I say to you that it shall be more tolerable for the land of Sodom in **the day** of judgment, than for you.

22) Matthew 12:36 And I say to you, that every careless word that men shall speak, they shall render account for it in **the day** of judgment.

23) Matthew 25:13 Be on the alert then, for you do not know **the day** nor the hour.

24) Luke 17:30 It will be just the same on **the day** that the Son of Man is revealed.

25) Romans 2:5 But because of your stubbornness and unrepentant heart you are storing up wrath for yourself in **the day** of wrath and revelation of the righteous judgment of God,

26) Romans 13:12 The night is almost gone, and **the day** is at hand. Let us therefore lay aside the deeds of darkness and put on the armor of light.

27) 1 Thessalonians 5:4 But you, brethren, are not in darkness, that **the day** should overtake you like a thief;

28) Hebrews 10:25 not forsaking our own assembling together, as is the habit of some, but encouraging *one another*; and all the more, as you see **the day** drawing near.

29) 2 Peter 1:19 And *so* we have the prophetic word *made* more sure, to which you do well to pay attention as to a lamp shining in a dark place, until **the day** dawns and the morning star arises in your hearts.

30) 2 Peter 2:9 *then* the Lord knows how to rescue the godly from temptation, and to keep the unrighteous under punishment for **the day** of judgment,

31) 2 Peter 3:7 But the present heavens and earth by His word are being reserved for fire, kept for **the day** of judgment and destruction of ungodly men.

32) 2 Peter 3:12 looking for and hastening the coming of **the day** of God, on account of which the heavens will be destroyed by burning, and the elements will melt with intense heat!

33) 1 John 4:17 By this, love is perfected with us, that we may have confidence in **the day** of judgment; because as He is, so also are we in this world.

Made in the USA
San Bernardino, CA
05 March 2017